Akkadian Grammar

SOCIETY OF BIBLICAL LITERATURE
Resources for Biblical Study

Edited by
Marvin A. Sweeney

Number 30
Akkadian Grammar

Translated by
HARRY A. HOFFNER, JR.

ARTHUR UNGNAD

AKKADIAN GRAMMAR

Fifth, corrected edition (1969)

Revised by
LUBOR MATOUŠ
The Charles University, Prague

Translated by
HARRY A. HOFFNER, JR.
The Oriental Institute of
The University of Chicago

Scholars Press
Atlanta, Georgia

Akkadian Grammar

Library of Congress Cataloging-in-Publication Data
Ungnad, Arthur, b. 1879.
[Grammatik des Akkadischen. English]
Akkadian grammar / by Arthur Ungnad; revised by Lubor Matous; translated by Harry A. Hoffner, Jr.
p. cm. — (Resources for biblical study; no. 30)
Includes index.
ISBN 1-55540-800-1 (cloth). — ISBN 1-55540-801-X (pbk.)
1. Akkadian language—Grammar. I. Matouš, Lubor. II. Title. III. Series.
PJ3251.U613 1993
492'.1—dc20 92-35712
CIP

Printed in the United States of America
on acid-free paper

Foreword to the Fourth Edition

W. von Soden's *Grundriss der akkadischen Grammatik*, published more than ten years ago, did not completely replace Arthur Ungnad's Assyro-Babylonian Grammar. As von Soden himself stresses, his *Grundriss* is not an ideal solution, because such a solution would need to serve both elementary instruction and research. In elementary instruction Ungnad's grammar is still used to this day, although it has been partially outdated by new discoveries. Most recently it was edited in a third edition after Ungnad's death by M. San Nicolò. Ungnad himself still chose the title for the third edition, *Grammatik des Akkadischen.* A fourth edition of his book needed to be thoroughly checked and brought into harmony with the present state of the discipline. This grammar of Akkadian is intended also to serve as an introduction to the ground-breaking grammar of W. von Soden.

In accordance with the wishes of the publisher, two viewpoints governed the production of the present fourth edition: Ungnad's method had to be preserved, and, where possible, the size of the preceding editions were not to be exceeded. But the necessary incorporation of the new discoveries that were for the first time systematically treated by von Soden (e.g., the perfect tense, semantic classes in the weak verbs, and various points of noun formation) required the addition of new sections and the elimination and rearrangement of other parts. Although Ungnad's grammar contained a section on syntax, he discussed many syntactical phenomena already in the morphology, such as the functions of the genitive. Thanks to von Soden's grammar, the structure of Akkadian syntax in many respects has become clearer, perhaps even for the first time clear. Therefore here too I had to reorganize the material and independently present the respective phenomena in the syntax section, which thereby naturally grew in size. This made it impossible to retain the paragraph numbering of Ungnad's grammar.

I was able to dispense with the separate exercise book that Ungnad appended to his grammar, since students today have access to Theo Bauer's *Akkadische Lesestücke* and more recently R. Borger's *Babylonisch-assyrische Lesestücke* (with a brief outline of Akkadian grammar). In addition K. Deller plans a Neo-Assyrian chrestomathy.

For literature and special questions on Akkadian grammar I refer the reader to the listing in von Soden's grammar, p. XII-XIV. Further important essays[1] and monographs, which have been published after the appearance of von Soden's *Grundriss*, are cited in the notes. Naturally it was not the task of the grammar to achieve completeness. Rather, new viewpoints, going beyond von Soden's work, were determinative. I should like to single out here the systematic treatment of Old Akkadian by I. J. Gelb in his *Old Akkadian Writing and Grammar* (MAD II),[2] which von Soden was not able to evaluate in his grammar. The Old Babylonian dialect has formed the basis for the present grammar, as for its predecessors,[3]

[1]See also I. J. Gelb, "Notes on von Soden's Grammar of Akkadian", BiOr XII (1955), 96ff.

[2]Issued in a second, revised and expanded edition (1961).

[3]Just as in the recently appeared "Grammatica della lingua Accadica" (Analecta Hierosolymitana 1, 1962) by A. Lancellotti and "Akkadskij

since Old Akkadian is to date still insufficiently understood and is therefore unsuitable as a basis for the presentation of grammatical phenomena.

I should like to express here my deepest gratitude to all who have supported me in my work, first of all to Professor W. von Soden, who read through my manuscript and improved it with valuable annotations. Professor K. Deller helpfully made his unpublished dissertation available to me and thereby acquainted me with the results of his latest research. Thanks to the friendly cooperation of Dr. K. Hecker, of Freiberg, I was able to use his still unpublished dissertation *Die Sprache der altassyrischen Texten aus Kappadokien*. Dr. J. Aro and Dr. B. Kienast furthered my work in many respects by their suggestions.

I am especially obligated to Professor R. Borger, who most kindly subjected the proofs of this grammar to a thorough checking and enriched them with important supplementary suggestions.

Prague, August 1964 L. Matouš

Foreword to the Fifth Edition

The present, fifth edition of the Grammar of Akkadian is fundamentally identical to the fourth. The most important improvements and suggestions of reviewers, for which I am very

---

jazyk" (Moscow 1964) by L. A. Lipin. (In contrast the "literary dialect [SB]" forms the basis of E. Reiner's structural grammar "A Linguistic Analysis of Akkadian" [1966].)

grateful to them, were incorporated as far as possible.[1] But the literature published since 1964, the year in which the fourth edition appeared, could only be utilized in exceptional cases, if the size of the book were to remain the same. I would like to express my sincere thanks again to Prof. R. Borger. In selfless cooperation he again thoroughly checked the correction sheets of the fifth edition and in many places suggested better formulations.

Prague, March 1968 L. Matouš

Translator's Preface

The prototype of this English translation was based upon the fourth edition of Ungnad–Matouš. It was prepared not for publication, but for classroom use during the years 1964–1974, while I was teaching Akkadian at Brandeis and Yale Universities. For such a purpose I was able both to dispense with the paradigms, which students consulted in the German edition, and to explain (in the text) grammatical phenomena differently than the authors, when this seemed preferable. But when in 1990 the editor of this series approached me about publishing my translation, I realized that such a book should be based upon the latest (fifth) German edition, and that it should either be thoroughly revised in keeping with all the important developments in the study of Akkadian since 1968, or purged of my classroom modifications and restored to the

---

[1] Especially the reviews of J. A. Brinkman, BiOr 23 (1966), 293ff., K. Deller, Or NS 34 (1965), 79ff. and J. Oelsner, OLZ 1969 (in press) [translator's note: see now OLZ 64 (1969) 33-35].

form of a strict translation of the fifth German edition. The second course has been chosen. Not even the bibliographical references in the footnotes have been updated, since this would logically lead to all sorts of additions of which there would be no end. The single exception concerns books that Matouš cited as in preparation, which have now appeared. For these I have provided the publication information.

I have permitted myself only a few necessary departures from the German edition. The abbreviations for the stages and dialects of the Akkadian language (OAkk, OB, etc.) follow the CAD rather than AHw. The semi-vowel that Ungnad–Matouš wrote as *j* is written here *y*. All paradigms at the end of the book have the same orientation. In the German editions the orientation varied from page to page, necessitating a constant turning of the book, when using the paradigms.

Some mechanical and typographical corrections have been made to the body of the text (e.g. the accidental dittography in § 88 b, section b), but especially to the indices of the 5th German edition, which sometimes did not correspond to the text of that edition.

I wish to thank those associates at The Oriental Institute who have generously assisted me in various ways. Professors John A. Brinkman and Walter Farber gave much helpful advice. Dr. Billie Jean Collins proofread the manuscript. Mr. Irving Diamond produced the index by computerized scanning. Dr. Thomas Holland, Thomas Urban and Richard Schoen of the Oriental Institute Publications Office gave valuable guidance in producing the camera-ready copy and kindly allowed me the use of their high-resolution laser printer. Of course, I take full responsibility for the final form of this translation.

Knowing how many students over the decades have benefited from “Ungnad”, it is my hope that this translation will make it even easier for English-speaking students to embark upon the fascinating study of the Akkadian language and its rich literature.

Chicago, September 1992 Harry A. Hoffner, Jr.

Table of Contexts

GRAMMAR

Introduction (§§ 1–3)

II. Morphology (§§ 25–99)

A. Pronouns (§§ 25-34)

II. The Stem Modifications (§§62-72)

III. Peculiarities Among Strong Verbs (§§ 74–76)

IV. The Weak Verbs (§§ 77–86)

E. Particles (§§ 88–99)

B. Verbs (XI–XXXVIII)

INDEX OF FORMS AND WORDS

List of Abbreviations

Bibliographical

AfO .... Archiv für Orientforschung
AHw .... W. von Soden, Akkadisches Handwörterbuch
ArOr .... Archiv Orientálni
AS .... Assyriological Studies
BAL .... R. Borger, Babylonisch-Assyrische Lesestücke (1963)
Bell .... Belleten
BiOr .... Bibliotheca Orientalis
CAD .... The Assyrian Dictionary of the Oriental Institute of the University of Chicago
DLZ .... Deutsche Literaturzeitung
GAG .... W. von Soden, Grundriss der akkadischen Grammatik
Iraq .... Iraq (Periodical)
JAOS .... Journal of the American Oriental Society
JCS .... Journal of Cuneiform Studies
JNES .... Journal of Near Eastern Studies
MAD .... Materials for the Assyrian Dictionary
Or NS .... Orientalia, Nova Series
RA .... Revue d'Assyriologie
RSO .... Rivista degli studi Orientali
SO .... Studia Orientalia
St. Op. .... Studies presented to A. L. Oppenheim (1964)
Syria .... Syria (Periodical)
WdO .... Die Welt des Orients
WZKM .... Wiener Zeitschrift für die Kunde des Morgenlandes
ZA .... Zeitschrift für Assyriologie

Other

abbrev.	abbreviated, abbreviation
acc.	accusative
adj.	adjective
adv.	adverb
Ass.	Assyrian
Bab.	Babylonian
c.	common (gender)
constr.	construct
dat.	dative
f.	feminine
fem.	feminine
gen.	genitive
imp.	imperative
indep.	independent
indic.	indicative
inf.	infinitive
interrog.	interrogative
LB	Late Babylonian
loc.	locative
m.	masculine
MA	Middle Assyrian
masc.	masculine
MB	Middle Babylonian
NA	Neo-Assyrian
NB	Neo-Babylonian
OA	Old Assyrian
OAkk	Old Akkadian
OB	Old Babylonian

parad.	paradigm
part.	participle
perf.	perfect
pers.	person
pl.	plural
prec.	precative
prepos.	preposition
pres.	present
pret.	preterite
pron.	pronoun
sg.	singular
st.	state
stat.	stative
subst.	substantive
suff.	suffix, sufformative
Sum.	Sumerian

GRAMMAR

INTRODUCTION

1. Relationship of Akkadian to Other Semitic Languages 1

Akkadian, which was so named by the inhabitants of Babylonia and Assyria themselves after the north Babylonian city Akkade, is the oldest Semitic language known to us. It branched off from a postulated Proto-Semitic language earlier than its sister languages and, under the influence of the prior language of the country, the non-Semitic Sumerian, developed in a peculiar fashion. Examples of this peculiar development are the loss of the laryngeals (cf. § 4e) and the position of the verb at the end of the sentence (cf. § 100c). The following table illustrates the position of Akkadian[5] within the Semitic languages: a

Proto-Semitic

West Semitic Group		East Semitic Group
Northwest-Semitic	Southwest-Semitic	
Ugaritic, Amorite, Hebrew, Phoenician Aramaic	North-Arabic, South Arabic, Ethiopic	Akkadian

The Semitic languages are distinguished from the (also inflected) Indo-European languages principally by the phenomenon that the meanings of words are bound up with a fixed sequence (the root), usually of three consonants (the radicals) (§ 51a). Every root has either a short (e.g., **prus, *pqid)* or a long (e.g. **kūn, *bnī)* root vowel, which is usually obscured by grammatical changes. The root **prus* (with the original root vowel *u)*, which in Akkadian always expresses the idea "to divide", is then more closely defined (in meaning) through vowels and affixed consonants (so-called "pre- b formatives", "afformatives" and rarely "infixes"). For example: $^{i}pr^{u}s$ "he divided", $p^{u}r^{u}ss^{\hat{u}}$ "decision", $^{i}p^{ta}r^{a}s$ "he has divided"; root **lba/iš* (with the original root vowel *a*, later *i*) "to clothe oneself"; $^{u\check{s}a}lb^{i}\check{s}$ " he clothed"; $l^{u}b^{u}\check{s}^{tu}$ "garment", $^{na}lb^{a}\check{s}^{u}$ "clothing".

2 **2. History of the Development of Akkadian**

a The oldest literary monuments in Akkadian come from southern Mesopotamia and originated in the middle of the third millennium, i.e., about 150 years before Sargon of Akkad (ca. 2350 BC according to the "low" chronology). We designate this oldest stage of the language Old Akkadian (OAkk). It lasts until about 1950. Not until the end of this period can we distinguish two principal dialects, the Babylonian (Bab.) in the south and the Assyrian (Ass.) in the north. The former finds its classical expression in the Old Babylonian (OB) of the time of King Hammurapi (1728–1686), especially in the language of the law code. Within OB several dialects can be distinguished: the two dialects of North- and South-Babylonia, the dialect of Mari[6], etc. The language of the contemporary hymns and epics, on the contrary, exhibits numerous archaisms. Old Assyrian documents and letters (OA) of the Assyrian merchant colonies[7] of the 18th century from eastern Asia Minor (esp. those found in Kültepe) stand closer to the Old Akkadian than does classical Babylonian.

b In the period after the close of the Hammurapi dynasty, the sources are at first quite sparse. The many connections that bound Babylonian to the related Assyrian resulted in a strong influence of the Babylonian dialect, which enjoyed the status of the scholarly language, on Assyria. Consequently, the language of the official Assyrian inscriptions of this period, as well as that of the Assyrian king Tiglath-pileser I (1112–1074), can scarcely be distinguished from Middle Babylonian (MB). Outside of the literary texts Middle Babylonian is also attested in letters and documents.[8] The Middle Assyrian language (MA) is to be found in the Assyrian law tablets from Assur, but is not totally free from Babylonian influences.

Note: The Akkadian employed ca. 1500–1200 in the peripheral areas (texts from Nuzi, Alalakh, Boghazköy, Ugarit, El Amarna, etc.) exhibits many peculiarities and irregularities due to a foreign linguistic substratum.

About 1000 B.C. the Akkadian language reached the stages that we designate as Neo-Babylonian (NB)[9] and Neo-Assyrian (NA). These dialects occur in pure form chiefly in documents and letters, which for both NB and NA are most abundantly preserved during the time of the Sargonids (ca. 722–609). Literary texts were transmitted and composed during this period in a more-or-less archaizing "high language" the so-called "Standard Babylonian" (SB) [Germ. "jungbabylonisch" (jB)]. Even the greater part of the so-called "Assyrian" royal inscriptions, esp. those of the Sargonids, is essentially SB, while only a very few of the earlier rulers, in particular Aššurnaṣirpal II[10] (883–859), sought to write in Neo-Assyrian. The confusion of the short-vowel endings (due to the dropping of final short vowels in speech) and ever stronger Aramaic influence are characteristic for Neo-Babylonian. Neo-Assyrian is somewhat better preserved, but exhibits numerous peculiarities due to independent development.[11] c

d The Chaldean Empire, which arose after the fall of Nineveh (612), brings us a large number of official and private documents, which clearly document the increasing Aramaicizing of the language. Chaldean kings such as Nebuchadnezzar II (604–562) considered the mimicking of archaic style in script and language as a worthwhile goal, but their efforts were often inadequate. Even after the capture of Babylon by Cyrus (539) Late Babylonian (LB) remained into the first pre-Christian century the literary and scholarly language, although it had long since been displaced as a spoken language by Aramaic.

e Without doubt beside the written language there was a vernacular, which only occasionally shines through the shrouding garment of the official language, for instance in private letters. In this grammatical outline we cannot pursue such questions further. We must also forego the attempt to characterize in detail the peculiar development of Assyrian in contrast to Babylonian. We shall restrict ourselves essentially to the Babylonian elements in Akkadian, especially as the majority of the Neo-Assyrian royal inscriptions must be regarded not as monuments of the Assyrian, but of the Babylonian branch of Akkadian. The reason for this predominance of Babylonian doubtless lay in the fact that through the centuries Babylon formed the center of intellectual life.

f *Note*: Obviously the numerous peripheral dialects of Akkadian, such as the Canaanite-influenced dialect of the El Amarna correspondence (EA), the Akkadian texts from the Hittite empire (Bogh), those from Ugarit (Ug.), the Babylonian texts from Elam,[12] and the Hurrian-influenced dialect of Nuzi, modern Kerkuk, are not taken into account here. Among other Semitic languages whose traces we can see in Akkadian, Canaanite influence on Old Babylonian, especially that of Mari, and Aramaic influence on NA and NB/LB, should be mentioned here.[13]

3. Paleography and Orthography 3

The cuneiform script that the Akkadians borrowed from the Sumerians consists partly of syllabic signs (*a, ab, ba, bab, baba,*[14] etc.) and partly of word signs or logograms,[15] (e.g. *šarrum*, "king"). Since one sign was often utilized for several syllabic and word values, the script requires a special study. One is accustomed to transcribe the text so that all the syllabic or word signs belonging to a word are joined by hyphens, e.g. *ālī-ya* (*āli* ideogram = "city" + *ya* = possessive suffix "my") or syllabically written (so-called transliteration) *a-li-ya*, read *ālīya*, "of my city". a

Syllables for which no special sign exists were split into two syllables, e.g. *pa-az*, read *paz* (not *paaz*); *pu-uz*, read *puz* (not *puuz*) Syllables for which syllabic signs do exist may also be expressed in this manner. One finds, for example, *ku-ur* (read *kur*, not *kuur*) written for *kur*. Thus, the same word will often appear in quite different forms, e.g. *šarrum* "king", ideographically *šarrum*, syllabically *šar-rum*, *ša-ar-rum*, *šar-ru-um*, *ša-ar-ru-um*, occasionally *šar-um*. — Signs are chosen so that the syllable boundaries cannot be misplaced, e.g. *i-par-ra-aš* (not, for instance, **ip-ar-aš*), read *iparraš*. Exceptions are found only at the beginning of individual suffixes, e.g. *aš-pur-ak-kum*, "I sent to you" (from *ašpur* + *akkum*) beside *aš-pu-ra-ak-kum*, both to be read *ašpurakkum*. b

When an *e* adjoins an *i*, the syllable is to be read with either an *e* or an *i*, e.g. ME-IL = *me-él* or *mì-il*, never *me-il*. Since, very often, the signs containing *i* also represent those c containing *e*, the decision whether to read *e* or *i* is often only possible on the basis of phonological rules, and even then, frequently almost impossible. So, for example, *el-li-it* is certainly to be read *ellet* (§ 5a), and one should transliterate it *el-le-et*.

d Double consonants (especially in older texts) are often not represented, as is equally true for long vowels: if the latter is to be designated, the vowel sign in question will be inserted, e.g. *ru-u-qu* (beside *ru-qu*), read *rūqu*; *re-e-qu* (beside *re-qu*; not to be read *ri-e-qu* or *ri-qu* respectively, see section c above), read *rēqu*.

e In Neo-Assyrian new orthographic principles have partially prevailed, such as the utilization of the sign with the phonetic value *bab* for bisyllabic *baba*, (cf. note above in § 3a) e.g. *i-*BAL-*kàt-u-ni*, read *i-bala-kàt-u-ni* (compare the writings: *i-ba-la-kàt-u-ni*).

f Akkadian does not have simple consonant signs (*b*, *d*, etc). Only with aleph, waw and yod is the vowel not differentiated.

ʾA = *ʾa, ʾi, ʾu* and *aʾ, iʾ, uʾ*

PI = *wa, wi, wu* and *aw, iw, uw*[16]

YA = *ya, yi, yu* and *ay*[17]

In the late period (probably under the influence of the Aramaic alphabetic writing) one can observe a tendency toward the formation of one- and two-consonant signs[18] that do not differentiate vowels. Compare, for example, the transliteration *li-qi-bu-ni* "let them say" instead of *liqbūni* (see also § 11b).

g Additional signs can be added to an logogram as endings, e.g. *šarru* "king", *šarru-u-tu* "kingship", read *šarrūtu*.

Akkadian has a series of determinatives, i.e., signs that appear before or after words of a specific class, without themselves being read. These are written in small type (in Sumerian) above the line, before or after the word in question. The most important determinatives are: ^{d}god (Sumerian dingir) before divine names, e.g. ^{d}Marduk = ^{god}Marduk; ^{uru}city; ^{kur}land; ^{íd}river; ^{lú}human (before names of professions or ethnic groups); ^{giš}wood (before tools, trees). The determinative before masculine personal names is represented by ^{I}(strictly speaking, the Roman numeral one) or ^{m}(masculine) or ^{P}(person); before feminine personal names by ^{f}(feminine) or ^{munus}woman, e.g. ^{I}*Bēlšunu* (a man's name). Common determinatives that occur after the word are the Sumerian words place^{ki}, e.g. Ur^{ki} (the city) Ur, and plant^{sar}, e.g. *karāšu*^{sar} "leek".[19] **h**

Phonetic complements often serve to fix the reading of an ambiguous logogram. Thus the same sign designates "god" and "heaven". If it is followed by the complement ^{lum}, *ilum* (*ilum*^{lum}) with the meaning "god" is intended to be read. But if ^{e} follows, *šamê* with the meaning "heaven" should be read. Like the determinatives, the phonetic complements are written in small letters above the line. Rarely do they occur after syllabic signs, as in *ak-šud*^{ud} (read *akšud*), and still more rarely before such, as in *um*-^{ma}*man* (read *umman*). **i**

For an illustration of the foregoing rules three sections from the Code of Hammurapi are given in syllabic (transliteration) and connected (transcription) writing. **j**

a) Transliteration:

§ 6 *šum-ma a-wi-lum* NÍG.GA DINGIR *ù* É.GAL *iš-ri-iq a-wi-lum šu-ú id-da-ak ù ša šu-ur-qá-am i-na qá-ti-šu im-ḫu-ru id-da-ak*

§ 128 *šum-ma a-wi-lum aš-ša-tam i-ḫu-uz-ma ri-ik-sa-ti-ša la iš-ku-un* MUNUS *ši-i ú-ul aš-ša-at*

§ 250 *šum-ma* GUD *sú-qá-am i-na a-la-ki-šu a-wi-lam ik-ki-ip-ma uš-ta-mi-it di-nu-um šu-ú ru-gu-um-ma-am ú-ul i-šu*

b) Transcription:

§ 6 *šumma awīlum namkūr ilim u ekallim išriq awīlum šū iddâk u ša šurqam ina qātīšu imḫuru iddâk*

§ 128 *šumma awīlum aššatam īḫuzma riksātīša lā iškun sinništum šī ul aššat*

§ 250 *šumma alpum sūqam ina alākīšu awīlam ikkipma uštamīt dīnum šū rugummâm ul īšu*

k Note 1: In transcription the circumflex denotes a long vowel resulting from the contraction of two vowels (e.g. *iddâk* "to be killed" < *iddūak*), while a macron represents other long vowels (e.g., *awīlum* "human being").

l Note 2: In transliteration, signs that have a similar phonetic value (called homophones) are distinguished by means of accents or small attached numbers (the system of François Thureau-Dangin, to which W. von Soden's "Das Akkadische Syllabar" of 1948 adheres), e.g. ša, šá, šà, ša$_4$, ša$_5$ (all to be read *ša*). Therefore these accents serve only to differentiate the signs and imply nothing about pronunciation.

Note 3: In the older language *ḫ* was often written for ʾ (cf. § 14b), e.g. OB *e-ḫi-il-tum* = *eʾiltum* "debt" (from *eʾēlum* "to bind"); OA *i-ḫi-id* = *iʾid* "beware" (root **nʾd*). **m**

Note 4: A. Falkenstein, Das Sumerische (1959), R. Labat, Manuel d'épigraphie akkadienne (1948, the fourth unrevised edition) and R. Borger, Babylonisch-assyrische Lesestücke, Heft 1-3 (1963) serve as an introduction to the writing system. **n**

I. PHONOLOGY (§§ 4-24)

A. PHONEMES 4

Akkadian possesses three basic vowels: *a, i, u*; and a secondary vowel *e* derived from either *a* or *i*. These all occur both short (*a, e, i, u)* and long (*ā, ē, ī, ū*, cf. § 3k).[20] Although no independent sign exists for *o* in the script, one can assume on the basis of the alternation of *u* and *a* (e.g., in NA *aš-par* "I sent" beside *aš-pur)* that this vowel too was known in Akkadian. In Greek transcriptions from a later period cuneiform *u* is often represented as *o*: σοβαθ = *šubat* "seat", νωρ = *nūr* "light".[21] Similarly, the vowel *ä* can be deduced from the alternation *a*/*e* or *a*/*i*.[22] Thus, for example, the NA writing *par*$^{\bar{a}}$/*īs* points to the pronunciation *parǟs* (cf. § 61a note). a

Genuine diphthongs are rare in Akkadian (§ 9c). When two different vowels follow one another in writing (except for *i-e, e-i*, cf. § 3c), they are almost always to be spoken separately (as in American English "re-use" and "theater"). b

Consonants: c

	voiced	voiceless	emphatic	nasal
dentals	d	t	ṭ	n
labials	b	p		m
palatals	g	k	q (velar)	
sibilants	z	s, š	ṣ	
liquids		l, r (tongue-r)		
laryngeals		ʾ (glottal stop)		
velar fricatives		ḫ		

The consonants *y* and *w* are semi-vowels in Akkadian. d

The original Semitic inventory of five laryngeals, i.e., ʾ$_1$ (= original aleph ʾ), ʾ$_2$ (= *h*), ʾ$_3$ (= *ḥ*), ʾ$_4$ (= ʿ), ʾ$_5$ (= *ġ*) were al- e ready reduced early in Akkadian.[23] All five sounds appear as glottal stop ʾ (aleph) in Akkadian from about 2000 B.C. In the earliest stratum of Old Akkadian (and partially also in OA), the leveling in alephs 3-5 (e.g., OAkk writings like *na-ʾà-aś*, "life of", where É (ʾ*à*) stands for original *ḥa*[24]), as well as the transition of *a* to *e* according to § 6a, e.g. *išma*ʾ$_4$ instead of the later *išme* "he heard", *ba*ʾ$_4$*ulātum* "the ruled (women)" (< *bêlum* "to rule", OA *be*ʾ*ālum*), had not taken place. Yet already in OAkk there are forms like *errēšum* "(tenant) farmer" beside *arrāšum*. Throughout the entire history of the Assyrian branch the change never took place in the verb *arāšum* "to sow" (cf. § 75h) — vs. Bab. *erēšum*[25] (cf. Arab. **ḥrṯ*).

f In older periods of Akkadian writing many sounds could not be represented unambiguously in writing. For instance, the emphatic sounds, for which there were no syllabic signs in Sumerian, were represented by the signs for similar sounding voiced and voiceless phonemes: *q* by *k*/*g*, *ṣ* by *z*, *ṭ* by *t*/*d*; even *s*/*š*/*z* and ʾ/*ḫ* could not be precisely distinguished from one another.

B. Changes in Sounds (§§ 5-22)

1. Vowels (§§ 5-11)

5 *a. Influence on Vowels by Other Vowels*

a In Babylonian, under the influence of a neighboring *e*-sound, an *a*-sound assimilates to the *e*-sound, whereas in Assyrian the *a*-sound remains unchanged: *bēlet* (§ 41b) "mistress of" (construct state), Ass. *bēlat*; *telqe* (§ 52f) "you took", Ass. *talqe*; *teleqqe* "you take", Ass. *talaqqe*. Even *ā* becomes *ē*: *epēšum* "to make", Ass. *epāšum*; *bēlēti* (§ 38f), Ass.

bēlāti; *erēbum* "to enter", Ass. *erābum*. An *e* that has thus arisen is often preserved through paradigmatic analogy (*Systemzwang*); cf. *telqû* (after *telqe*). In MB and NB, *e* for *a* is often found in preterites of D- and Š- stems: *ubenni* "he made (it) beautiful" for *ubanni*; *ureppiš* "he made (it) broad" beside *urappiš*; *ušekniš* "he subdued" beside *ušakniš*. This is probably due to partial assimilation of the *a* to the *i* of the following syllable (§ 65c). Through regressive assimilation in the *e*-containing verbs, the *a* of the prefixes *a*- and *ta*- becomes *e*, e.g. *ešemme* "I hear", *tešebber* "you break" (see § 52 f).

In Ass., a short unaccented *a* in the next to last syllable of the word assimilates to the vowel in the final syllable (the so-called "Assyrian vowel-harmony"): *iṣbutū* "they seized" (Bab. *iṣbatū)*; *qaqqurum* "ground" (nom.), *qaqqirim* (gen.), *qaqqaram* (acc.) (for Bab. *qaqqarum, qaqqarim, qaqqaram*); *libbu-šu* "his heart", *libbi-ki* "your (f. sg.) heart", *libba-ša* "her heart" (vs. Bab. *libba*- in all three cases; cf. § 42d). Less frequently without vowel assimilation: *uṭṭatim* "grain" (gen. sg. of *uṭṭutum)*. Forms like *ṭuppa-šunu* "their tablet", *tērta-kunu* "your (pl.) reply" are not true exceptions, since the *a* in this case is neither unaccented nor in the next to last syllable of the word. Cf. § 42d. b

Note 1: Through analogy, at times even in forms with *i* and *u* as theme vowels, to which the unaccented *a* in the preceding syllable has assimilated, the assimilated form will be retained after the loss of the theme vowel through elision. Examples: *iššiknū* (§ 66a), "they were placed" (< **iššikinū* < **inšákinū*; Bab. *iššaknū)*; *issuḫra* (NA) "he turned himself about" (<**issuḫura* <**istaḫura*; Bab. *issaḫra)*. Yet note OA *ētatqū* (G-stem perf.) "they have passed" beside sg. *ētitiq* (§ 77h). c

d *Note* 2: Occasionally even a long, accented *a* will undergo Ass. vowel harmony, e.g. OA *pū-šū* "his mouth" (from *pāʾum*), *pā-ša, pī-ki*. Often the same holds true for *a* in a positionally long (i.e., a closed) syllable, e.g. OA *ana išrī-šu* "to his place" (from *ašrum*), MA *ina idre* "on the threshing floor" (from *adru*).[26]

6 *b. Influence on Vowels by Consonants*

a *a* becomes *e* under the influence of one of the sharp laryngeals, alephs 3 (PS *ḥ*), 4 (PS ʿ), and sometimes 5 (PS ǵ), which are leveled to glottal stop (aleph) (§ 4e): *ēpuš* "I made" from earlier $a{ʾ}_4$*puš*; *bēlum* "lord" from *ba*$ʾ_4$*lum*.

b Often *i* becomes *e* under the influence of *ḫ* and *r*: *umaʾʾer* "I commissioned", *utammeḫ* "I grasped". Under certain circumstances in later Assyrian, for instance in the genitive and in the ventive ending *-nim*, the final *-im* becomes *-e* (*šanīte* "of the other", for *šanītim*) (cf. § 58a).

c In Bab. *a* before or after *r* can become *e*, which often produces a vowel assimilation in the neighboring syllable, e.g. *šebērum* "to smash" for **šabārum*; *qerēbum* "to approach" for (Ass.) *qarābum*.

7 *c. Elision of Vowels Between Consonants*

a Short unstressed vowels between single consonants are often elided, unless a long vowel stands before the preceding consonant. This protects the unstressed vowel, as does the doubling of this consonant, e.g. **parisum* becomes *parsum*, but *pārisum* remains unchanged; *iptarasū* becomes *iptarsū*, but *iparrasū* remains unchanged.

b If the short vowel in question immediately precedes an *r*, it will sometimes fail to elide: *zikarum* beside *zikrum* "man", *šikarum* "beer", *laberum* "old".

d. Reduction of Long Vowels 8

Final long vowels that do not owe their length to contraction of two earlier short vowels under certain circumstances can be shortened (cf. § 23). Notable examples are the originally long vowels of the Final Weak Verbs (cf. § 83a), such as *imnu* "he counted" instead of *imnū*, *ibni* "he built" instead of *ibnī*, *imla* "he was full" instead of *imlā*. Likewise long vowels in a closed syllable (§ 23), e.g. *liprus* < *lū iprus* (§ 60a). a

When suffixes are added to these forms, the originally long vowels are preserved: *ibnī-šu*, "he built it". b

e. Contraction of Vowels 9

Vowels that — as a result of the loss of the glottal stop (aleph), or the semi-vowels *w* or *y* — came into direct contact with each other, were contracted (earlier in Babylonian than in Assyrian). Usually in such cases the short vowel is swallowed up by the following long vowel, e.g. *anniūtum* "these" (uncontracted OB and OA) later contracted to *û* (§ 3k): *annûtu(m)*; *qibiānim* "say to me" (often still uncontracted in OB and Ass.) contracted in later Bab. to *â*: *qibâni*. On the other hand, short *e* followed internally by *ā* contracted in Bab. to *ê*: *beʾālum* (OA) "to rule", *bêlum* (Bab.). Two adjacent short vowels produce a long one, which usually has the quality of the second: *rabûm* "large" from *rabium*, *rabâm* (acc.) from *rabiam* (so written in older Bab. and Ass., where contraction had not yet occurred in all cases), *šadûm* "mountain" from **šaduʾum*. In NA two vowels in direct contact in the final position remain uncontracted,[27] e.g. *anniu* "this", *qibiam* "say to me", *iqabbiū* "they say". In the Mari dialect *i* and *a* a (*ā*) = *ê*, e.g. *kêm* "thus", Bab. *kiʾam*; *nêti* (§ 25d:17) "us" (acc.), Bab. *niāti*; *iqêš* "he bestows", Bab. *iqīaš* or *iqâš* (§ 82g).

b If the first of the two vowels is long, then either (1) both vowels remain uncontracted, esp. in the older language (OAkk, OA) (always in the G participle of the hollow roots, e.g. *dāʾikum* "killing"), or (2) they contract, e.g. *rubāʾum* "prince", Bab. *rubûm*; *qabāʾim* (gen. inf.) "of blessing", later (beginning in MB and MA) *qabê*.

c The original Semitic diphthongs *ai* and *au* were monophthongized in Akkadian: *ai* becomes Bab. *ī*, Ass. *ē*, e.g. *bītum* (Ass. *bētum*); *au* becomes *ū* in both dialects, e.g. *mūtum* "death" from **mautum*.

10 *f. Crasis*

The fusion of the final vowel of a preceding word with the initial vowel of the word that follows (crasis) is seldom indicated in the written language: e.g. *la-ma-ri* beside *la a-ma-ri* "of not seeing", *ša-wa-at* beside *ša a-wa-at* "of the word", *i-nu-mi-šu* "at that time" (actually "in its day") instead of *ina ūmī-šu, inammitim* (OA) "according to the cubit" beside *ina ammitim*. Also in OA, names — such as *Issurik* (from **id-šu-arik* "his hand is long"). Crasis always takes place with the wish particle *lū* in the precative (cf. § 60a).

11 *g. Interpolation of Vowels*

a Interpolation of vowels often serves to resolve consonantal clusters, esp. at the end of a word in the construct state (§ 41d), e.g. *kalab* "dog of" for **kalb, uzun* "ear of" for **uzn*, or with consonantal clusters at the beginning of the G-stem imperative (§ 63e), e.g. *kušud* "reach!" from **kšud, ṣabat,* "seize!" from **ṣbat*. This interpolated vowel usually corresponds to the vowel of the neighboring syllable.

Often in OA before the liquids *l*, *r*, and even *m* and *n* there appear epenthetic vowels, which are probably to be explained from the vocalic aspect[28] of these consonants. To a certain extent they are not subject to Ass. vowel harmony (§ 5b), e.g. *šukunā* "place!" beside *šuknā, bīt wabirī* "guest house" instead of *bīt wabrī, ṭuppū ḫarrumūtum*[29] "tablets (enclosed) in the envelope", for the sg. *ṭuppum ḫarmum.* b

On the other hand, such epenthetic vowels in the later language (NA, LB),[30] e.g. *uzunā-šu* "his (two) ears", and quite rarely forms like *šuḫumuṭu* "to fetch quickly" = *šuḫmuṭu*, should be explained as orthographic and due to Aramaic influence. c

2. Semi-Vowels (§§ 12-13)[31]

a. The Semi-Vowel w 12

In MB and later times initial *w* is regularly lost, e.g. *wašib* "he dwells", SB *ašib*. Often in OA and always in later Ass. *wa-* becomes *u-*, e.g. *urad* "slave" (constr. state), beside *warad*; *urḫu(m)* "month" = Bab. *(w)arḫum*; *urkatam* "later" beside *warkatam*. a

Intervocalic *w* is written in MB and later as *m*, e.g. *amīlu* "man", older *awīlum* (in MA sometimes not even written, cf. *aʾīlu* instead of *awīlu*). In later Assyrian some *m*'s intervocalically shift to (written) *b*: *abutu* "word" = *amātu*, older *awātum*; *labû* "to encircle" = Bab. *lawûm*, later *lamû.* b

Note: Initial *w* becomes *b* in the root **wbl* because of the following *b*: inf. *babālum* "to carry" = *wabālum*, N-stem pres. *ibbabbal* (§ 80f, k).

c At the end of a syllable *w* fuses with the preceding vowel to form either a long vowel or the diphthong *au*, which further develops to *ū*: *ūšib* "I sat" from **awšib*.

Note: a *w* sometimes develops secondarily as a hiatus indicator (cf. also § 13b note) between the two vowels, Ass. *itūwar* "he turns back" beside *itūar* (cf. § 82g).

13 *b. The Semi-Vowel* y

a *y* is very rarely preserved in initial position, notably in the pronominal forms of the first person singular (*yâšim, yâti, yāum).* The original verbal prefix *ya*- becomes *i*-, *yu*- becomes *u*-; e.g. **yaprus* becomes *iprus* (§ 52e), **yuparris* becomes *uparris*.

Note: The continuation of the distinction between **ʾu*- and **yu*- in OAkk verbal prefixes[32] can most probably be detected by the employment of the cuneiform homophonic signs *ú* and *ù* for the 1 sg. **ʾu*, and the sign *u* for the 3 sg./pl. **yu*. Verbs that were originally I *y* developed from *ya*- to *e*- in the infinitive forms, e.g. *ešērum* "to be in order" from **yašārum*.

b Internal, post-vocalic *y* is only in the possessive suffix *-ya*, e.g. *bēlī-ya* (gen.) "of my lord" (§ 26c, 2). But after *ū* the *y* of the possessive suffix *-ya* usually becomes ʾ: *bēlū-a* "my lords". Also otherwise the script often does not indicate *y* after a long vowel: *qātā-ʾa* beside *qātā-ya, šēpē-ʾa* beside *šēpē-ya*. *y* assimilates to immediately preceding *n* in N-stem verbal forms, e.g. *innešer* (§ 81d).

Note: In NA *y* can be inserted — as *w* is in OA (§ 12c, note) — to mark a hiatus between two adjacent vowels,[33] e.g. *anniu* (*anniyu*).

3. Consonants (§§ 14-21)

14 *a. Laryngeals* (ʾ)

a The glottal stop ʾ (aleph) (cf. § 4e) is normally not represented in the writing, when it occurs initially. The verbs with initial aleph are an exception to this rule, for in OB forms of the G present and D present and preterite the initial glottal stop is represented in the script through the prefixing of a pleonastic vowel sign which is the same as the vowel that immediately follows the aleph (cf. § 75b), e.g. *i-ik-ka-al* (read *ʾikkal*) and *u-ub-bi-it* (read *ʾubbit*). But compare also writings such as *i-in* (OB) or *e-en* (OA) "eye of", etc.

In the older stages of the language the glottal stop occurring internally was variously represented in the script: (1) through unusual distribution of the syllabic signs, e.g. *iš-al* (instead of *i-ša-al*) to represent *išʾal* "he asked"; (2) through the employment of a superfluous, homophonous vowel sign, e.g. *lu-uḫ-ri-a-am* (*a* for *ʾa*), to be read *luḫriʾam* "let me dig up"; (3) through the use of *ḫ*-containing syllabic signs (cf. § 3m), e.g. *e-ḫi-il-tum* (OB), to be read as *eʾiltum* "indebtedness", *ú-na-aḫ-ḫi-id* (OA) to be read *unaʾʾid* "he reported". The *ḫ*-containing signs can thus serve to render all of the proto-Semitic laryngeals (cf. § 4e). b

Post-consonantally, glottal stop is usually lost and replaced by compensatory lengthening of the preceding vowel: *ḫīṭum* "sin" from *ḫiṭʾum*; *mīlum* "flood waters" from **milʾum*. In later stages of the language consonantal doubling occasionally replaced compensatory lengthening: *ḫiṭṭu* (cf. § 22b) beside *ḫīṭu*. In the I ʾ verbs the ʾ usually assimilates to the preceding consonant: *innabit* "he fled" from *inʾabit* (§ 75g). In forms of the root **ʾlk* (proto-sem. *hlk*) the ʾ will assimilate to a consonant that immediately follows it: *illik* "he went" from **iʾlik* (§ 75c). c

At the end of a syllable, glottal stop is replaced by compensatory lengthening of the syllable vowel: *zību* "jackal" d from **zi*ʾ*bu*; *ākul* "I ate" from **a*ʾ*kul* (§ 75b); *bēlum* "lord" from **ba*ʾ*lum*. In Ass. *i*ʾ becomes *ē* in cases like *ērub* "he entered".

15 ***b. Dentals*** **(d, t, ṭ)**

a *d* assimilates to an immediately following *t*, and in certain circumstances even to an *š*: *ma*ʾ*attu* "much" from **ma*ʾ*adtu*, f. of *ma*ʾ*adu* (cf. § 15c); *eššu* "new" from **edšu* .

b In MB and later *d* assimilates to *n*: *innā* from *idnā* "give!"; *ittannū* (perf. of *ndn*) from **ittadnū* (§ 78e).

c In Late Ass. *lt* becomes *ss*: *isseqe* "he took" (rare) from *ilteqe* (*lq*ʾ); *batussu* "virgin" from *batultu*. *tt* in NA becomes *ss* (cf. § 20b) in *ma*ʾ*assu* = *ma*ʾ*adtu* "much" (§ 15a).

d In forms with infixed *-ta-* (perf. tense and forms of the *t*-stems) *t* becomes:

(a) *d* after *g* or *d*: *igdamrū* (§ 74gα) "they completed" (**gmr*); *iddūk* (§ 82g) " he killed" (**dwk*). In later Bab. even after *m*: *amdaḫiṣ* "I fought" (**mḫṣ*); thus occasionally even in the f. ending of nouns (§ 37c): *tâmdu* "sea" = *tâmtu*; *rušumdu* "swamp" = *rušumtu*;

(b) *ṭ* after *ṭ*: *aṭṭardam* "I have now sent" from perf. *aṭtardam*; in Ass. even after *q* (actually contrary to the law of the incompatibility of the emphatic consonants; cf. § 21b); *iqṭibi* "he said" (Bab. *iqtabi*);

(c) assimilated to all preceding sibilants except *š* (cf. § 20b): *aṣṣabat* "I seized" (perf.) from *aṣtabat* (§ 74d); *izzakar* "he named" from **iztakar*.

e *Note*: in NA one observes a tendency to pronounce the voiceless *t* as *d*, e.g. Bab. *galātum* "to terrify", NA *galādu*.

c. The Dental Nasal n 16

The *n* that is to be expected initially in imp., inf., and stative of Ntn is dropped: *itapras* from **nitapras*. a

Syllable-closing *n* assimilates to the following consonant: *iddin* "he gave" from **indin* (§ 78b); in N: *ipparis* "he was divided" from **inparis*; in the iterative stems: when the *-tan-* infix stands before consonants (§ 70b), *iptarras* (pret. Gtn from **ip-tan-ras*). Very often also in OA after apocopated prepositions *an(a)* and *in(a)*: *aṣṣēr* = *an(a)* + *ṣer* "over and above that"; *iṣṣer* (§ 80b) = *in(a)* + *ṣer* "to the charge of". Cf. also Bab. *akkâšim* (§ 25e) "to you" from *an(a) kâšim*. b

Note: Beside the dental *n* there was also — to be sure, though not represented by a distinctive cuneiform sign — a palatal *n̊*, as can be deduced from the free variation of *m* and *n* before dentals: *ina*^{n}*/mdin* " he gives" (from *inaddin*) — pronounced probably *ian̊din* (§ 22c). c

*d. Labials (*b, p*)* 17

b can assimilate to an immediately following *m*: *ērum-ma* "he entered and ..." from *ērub-ma*; *uššam-ma* "he sits down and ..." from *uššab-ma* (§ 80c). a

After *š* as the result of a partial assimilation, *b* sometimes becomes *p*: NA *uspākūni* "(where) I dwell" = Bab. *wašbāku*, beside *usbakūni*; even OB *šupat* (stat. constr.) "dwelling of" beside *šubat*. b

Note 1: In NA and to a certain extent even in MA (cf. writings like *api* "my father" for *abī*) the voiced/voiceless distinction in the labials seems to have been totally blurred.[34] c

Note 2: From the spelling variations *b*/*w* in *ḫuwul* / *ḫubul* "debt of" a spirantized pronunciation of the *b* can be posited for OA. Compare also OAkk writings with *b* for *w*: *baqartum* (f.) "valuable" for *waqartum*, and *abīlīya* (gen.) "of my man" for *awīlī-ya* .

18 **e. *The Labial Nasal* m**

a The nominal preformative *m^a/e-* (§ 36h), when prefixed to roots containing a labial, becomes *n^a/e-* ("Barth's law"), e.g. *napḫarum* "total" (instead of **mapḫarum*).

b Especially in NA, intervocalic, etymological *m* (pronounced *w*) often becomes ʾ or disappears entirely in the writing, whereupon contraction takes place: MA *daʾiqu*, NA *deʾiq*, *dêq* from *damiq* "is good"; *Dûzu* "Tammuz" beside *Duʾuzu* from *Dumuzu*, cf. *šepūʾa* from **šēpum-ya* "at my feet".

c In the final position any *m* that is not part of the root will be lost, mostly in MB and MA, especially evident in the loss of mimation in the noun (39b), in pronominal dative forms (§§ 25c and 26b) and in the ventive (§ 58). What in later periods appears to be mimation is intentional archaizing.

d The final *m* of the locative adverbial in *-um* (§ 44d) and of the ventive assimilates to the consonant that begins the following suffix: *šēpuš-šu* (from **šēpum-šu)* "at his foot"; *ašpurak-kum* (from **ašpuram-kum)* "I sent to you"; Ass. *ša iddinanni* from **iddinam-ni* "which he gave to me".

e Before dentals (§ 15) as well as *š, ṣ, q,* and *k* (rarely other sounds) *m* that is part of the root sometimes (from MB on) becomes *n*: *enqu* (SB) "wise" beside *emqum* (**ʾmq)*; *ṭēn-ka* (NA) "your command" from *ṭēm-ka*; *mundaḫṣī* (MB, LB) "warriors" (**mḫṣ*); *anši* (MB) "I forgot" (= *amši)*; *ḫanša*[35] (MB) "five" (= *ḫamša)*. This secondary *n* then assimilates in NA according to § 16b: *attaḫar* (§ 74eα) "I received" from **antaḫar* (**mḫr)*; rarely in Bab.: *šaššāniš* "like the sun" (from **šamšum)*; *šuššu* "his name" from *šum-šu*; OA *ḫaššat* (f.) "five" from *ḫamšat*.

Note: For assimilation of *m* in OA see *aḫḫur* (wr. *a-ḫu-ur*, < **mḫr*) "I received".[36]

f. Liquids (l, r) 19

a For the shift from *lt* to *ss* in Assyrian cf. § 15c.

b Total assimilation of *l* and *r* to the following consonant is attested particularly in NA, cf. *bīt* from *bi(r)t* "where", *iššaššûme* "on the third day" (*ina šalše ūme*), *annabu* "hare" (= *arnabu*).[37]

c For the shift from *i* to *e* before *r* cf. § 6b.

d Before a dental in NB *r* often becomes *š*: *šipištu* "message" = *šipirtu*; *Urašṭāya* "Urartian" = *Urarṭāya*.

e Sporadically, *r* takes the place of *š* before a dental, cf. *irdud* "he dragged" instead of *išdud*.

Note 1: The alternation between *r* and *š* allows us to conclude that there was a Bab. phoneme *ř* (like the Czech *ř*). That the divine name *Ninurta* contained this sound may be deduced from the Aramaic spelling *Inušta*.[38]

Note 2: On the epenthetic vowels before *l* and *r* cf. § 11b.

g. Sibilants (z, s, ṣ, š) 20

a Akkadian distinguishes the following sibilants[39]: a voiced *z*, a voiceless *s*, an emphatic *ṣ* and a palatal *ś* (still discernible in the older stages of the language), which in OB has already merged with *š*. *ś* is found, for instance, in the personal pronouns of the third person (§§ 25-26) and in causal preformative *śa* -.

b From MB and MA on, all four sibilants *z, s, ṣ, š* become *l* before a dental or sibilant: *alṭur* "I wrote" beside *ašṭur* (**šṭr*); *alsi* "I called" beside *ašsi* (*šsy*), in OA on the contrary *issi* "he called" (§ 74dα). *š* is often preserved before the *t* of the feminine ending (§ 37c), e.g. *napištum* "life" beside *napultum*. In

NA the *lt* that arises from *št* further develops to *ss* according to § 15c: *assakan* = *aštakan* (Bab. *altakan*).

Note: under certain circumstances *ṣt* can become *št*: cf. OB *maruštum*, f. of *marṣum* "ill", *ištum*, f. to *īṣum* "few, little".[40]

c *š* of the pronominal suffixes (§ 26b) regularly becomes *s* (§ 86d) after the dentals and sibilants. The dental or sibilant then assimilates to the following *s* (which developed from *š*) resulting in *ss*: *mās-su* (frequently spelled *mat-su*) "his land" from **māt-šu*; *bēlūs-su* "his lordship" from **bēlūt-šu*; *imḫas-su* "he smote him" from **imḫaṣ-šu*; *erēs-su* "his desire" from *erēš-šu*. In OA on the other hand the sequence *šš* is always preserved, e.g. *lubūš-šunu* "their clothing", *tēriš-šum* "you requested for him". In OB the two sibilants were still differentiated: *ulabbiš-šu* "she clothed him" (original final *ś*) versus *epussunūši* "do for them" (final *š*).

d Later Ass. has *s* in place of Bab. *š* before *b*/*p*: *uspāku* (§ 17b) "I sit" compared with Bab. *wašbāku*; *ina sapal* "beneath" (beside *ina šapal*). The Assyrians pronounced Bab. *š* like an *s*; it appears as though NA *s* always stands for the etymological palatal *ś* of OAkk.[41]

21 *h. The Emphatic Consonants and Velar* q

a Although two emphatic consonants in the same root can be tolerated in other Semitic languages, in Akkadian one of them dissimilates (i.e., loses its emphatic quality): *ṭ* – *q*/*ṣ* becomes *t* – *q*/*ṣ*; *q* – *ṣ* becomes *k* – *ṣ*; *q* – *ṭ* becomes *q* – *t* ("Geers' Law"), e.g. *kaṣārum* "to join together, unite" (cognate to Heb. **qṣr*); *qatnum* "thin" (cf. Heb. **qṭn*). In OB beside *qaqqadum* "head" the form *kaqqadum* is attested, beside *qaqqarum* "ground" the forms *kaqqarum* and *kakkarum* are also attested.[42]

A seeming exception to Geers' Law in NA is *iqṭibi* (§ 15d) **b**
"he said" (perf.) with partial assimilation of the *t* to the emphatic *q*. But this exception is only apparent, because Geers' Law concerns only the tolerance of emphatics in the *root*, not in the grammatical affixes.

i. Doubled Consonants **22**

Doubled consonants in many cases are written as single **a**
ones, especially in older texts (regularly in OAkk and OA). Doubled consonants in final position are simplified, e.g. *dān* (written plene *da-a-an*) "he is strong" from **dann*; *šar* (constr. state) "king" from **šarr*.

Doubled consonants are either original — as in D-stem **b**
(*uparras*, *uparris*, etc.) or secondary. They can arise secondarily through the total assimilation of one consonant to another, e.g. *iddin* "he gave" from **indin* (*ndn*; cf. §78b), or through a compensatory lengthening: *ḫiṭṭu* "sin" from *ḫīṭu* (compensatory lengthening for *ḫīṭʾu*; § 14c). Through accent displacement consonantal doubling sometimes takes place, especially in Bab.:[43] *i-din-nam* = *iddínnam* < *íddinam*; *tašpúrram* from *tášpuram* "you sent to me".

Doubled consonants, esp. *bb, dd, gg, zz* (i.e., voiced ones), **c**
in Bab. are often resolved into *m* + labial, or *n* + dental or sibilant (nasalization): *ina*^{m}*/ndin* from *inaddin* "he gives"; *ambi* (**nbʾ* § 84e) "I called" beside *abbi*; *inanziq* from *inazziq* "he becomes vexed". All this seems to point to a palatal nasal *n̊* (but not a distinct phoneme, only an allophone) for which no separate cuneiform sign was available (§ 16c).

d *Note*: Regarding the shift from *tt* to *ss* in *maʾattu maʾassu* cf. § 15c.

4. Syllables and Accent (§§ 23-24)

23 ### *j. Syllables*

There are two syllable types: open (V or CV) and closed (VC or CVC). A closed syllable with a short vowel (CVC) is considered as a long syllable. An open syllable with a long vowel (CV̄) is also considered a long syllable. Final long vowels and long vowels in closed syllables are often shortened in Akkadian (§ 8a).

24 ### *k. Accent*

a The word stress lies on the long ultima, if this has arisen through contraction of two short vowels: *maḫrûm* "first" from *maḫrīum*; otherwise, in bisyllabic words the stress falls on the penult (e.g., *kúšud* "reach!"), on the antepenult in polysyllabic words when the penult contains a short vowel (e.g., *íprusū* "they divided"). When endings are added to the word, the word stress falls on the syllable preceding these endings, e.g. *iprusū́nim* contrasted with *íprusū*.

b Since the construct (§ 41) forms an accentual unit with the following genitive, and thus in a sense a single word (§ 41a), the construct bears only a secondary stress, e.g. *šàmšu Bā́b-ili* "the sun of Babylon". Monosyllabic construct forms (*bīt ílim)* probably bear no stress at all.

c The vowel of the genitive before the pronominal suffix was most likely lengthened as a result of accent displacement, since constructions like *ina ṣērī-ki* "to you" in poetry often occur at the end of the verse, where one would normally expect a trochee.[44] See also below § 42a.

In sentence questions the sentence stress falls on the last lengthened syllable of the word that is the object of the question. Thus, for example, the substantivized neuter interrogative pronoun *mīnu(m)* (§ 31a), as a result of the interrogative stress, occurs with a long final vowel, *minû(m)*. **d**

II. MORPHOLOGY (§§ 25–99)

A. PRONOUNS (§§ 25-35)

1. Personal Pronouns (§§ 25-27)

There are independent and suffixed pronouns. The latter may be added to the noun or the verb.

a. Independent Personal Pronouns 25

In the strict sense of the word, Akkadian possesses per- a
sonal pronouns only for the first and second person singular and plural. According to its function, the third person pronoun is an anaphoric pronoun and, when used adjectivally, should be rendered as "the afore-mentioned" or "that one", e.g. *sinništum šī* "that woman". The independent personal pronouns and the anaphoric pronoun each exhibit three case forms: nom., gen./acc., and dat. (also after the prep. *ana)*. The dat. forms are expanded with *š*, the acc. forms with *t*.

In later periods the *š*- and *t*-forms were often confused. In b
OA the gen./acc. forms were also employed for the dative.

c

	nom.	dat.[1]	gen./acc.[2]
Sg. 1 c	*anāku*	*yâši(m)*[3]	*yâti*
2 m	*attā*[4]	*kâši(m)*[5]	*kâti/a*[6]
2 f	*attī*[7]	*kâši(m)*	*kâti*[8]
3 m	*šū*[9]	*šuāšim*[10]	*šuāti/u*[11]
3 f	*šī*[12]	*šiāšim*[13]	*šiāti*[14]
Pl. 1 c	*nīnu*[15]	*niāšim*[16]	*niāti*[17]
2 m	*attunu*[18]	*kunūši(m)*[19]	*kunūti*[20]
2 f	*attina*[21]	*kināši(m)*[22]	*kināti*[23]
3 m	*šunu*[24]	*šunūši(m)*[25]	*šunūti*[26]
3 f	*šina*[27]	*šināši(m)*[28]	*šināti*[29]

Note 1: Annotations. **1.** Not OA. **2.** In OA also used for the dat. (cf. d
§ 25b). **3.** Later forms: *yâšu/a*. **4.** The first *t* assimilated from *n* (**antā*) (§ 16b). **5.** Late *kâšu*. **6.** In OA *ku(w)āti* (cf. § 12c note). **7.** Assimilated

from **anti*. **8.** In OA *ku(w)āti* (cf. note 6) is also f. **9.** OAkk *śu*, OA *šūt*, NA *šūtu*. **10.** Or *šâšu(m)*. **11.** Or *šâtu/i*; OAkk *śua*, later *šuāti*. **12.** OAkk *śī*, OA *šīt*, NA *šīti*. **13.** In OB *šuāši(m)* also for f. Later *šâši/a*. **14.** Or *šâti*, in OB also *šuāti* like the m. **15.** From **naḫnu*. Later form *anēnu*, Ass. *nēnu*. **16.** Later *nâši*. **17.** In Mari: *nêti* (cf. § 9a). **18.** From **antunu*. **19.** Later *kâšunu*. **20.** Later *kâtunu*. **21.** From **antina*. **22.** Later *kâšina*. **23.** Later *kâtina*. **24.** OAkk *śunu*. **25.** Later *šâšunu*. **26.** Later *šâtunu*; OAkk *śunūti*. **27.** OAkk *śina*. **28.** Later *šâšina*. **29.** Later *šâtina*.

e *Note* 2: The gen./acc. forms also follow the prepositions (except for *ana*, which governs the dative, e.g. *ana kâšim* "to you", also with assimilation *akkâšim*, cf. § 16b): *ša kīma yâti* "he who (is) as I", i.e., "my agent"; *ela yâti* "except for me" (cf. § 88b sub f). In OA third pers. sg. fem. is also used in a neuter sense: *aššiāti* "because of which" from *ana šiāti*, for which in OB *ana šuāti*, MB/SB *ana šatti*.[45]

f *Note* 3: The independent dative and acc. forms are principally employed to emphasize the personal pronoun, in which cases the corresponding pronominal suffix (§ 26b) is also appended to the verb, e.g. *yâti īzibanni* "he abandoned *me*", *ana šuāšim šaṭer-šum* "to *him* is written"; *kunūti ḫabbulak-kunūti* (OA) "he is in *your* (pl.) debt".

26 *b. Pronominal Suffixes*

a The pronominal suffixes are appended to both nouns and verbs: (1) The genitive forms appended to nouns serve principally to express the possessive relationship. (2) The dative and acc. forms appended to the verbs mark the indirect or direct objects. Later the dat. and acc. suffixes merge, so that the various forms frequently are no longer strictly distinguished.

b

	gen.	dat.	acc.
sg. 1 c	*-ī*[1], *-(y)a*[2]	*-a(m)*[3], *-ni(m)*[4]	*-ni, -ī*[4a]
2 m	*-ka*	*-ku(m)*	*-ka*
2 f	*-k(i)*[5]	*-ki(m)*	*-ki*
3 m	*-š(u)*[5]	*-šu(m)*	*-š(u)*[6]
3 f	*-š(a)*[5]	*-ši(m)*	*-š(i)*[6]
Pl. 1 c	*-ni*[7]	*-niāši(m)*[8]	*-niāti*[8]
2 m	*-kun(u)*[5]	*-kunūši(m)*[9]	*-kunūti*[10]
2 f	*-kin(a)*[5]	*-kināši(m)*[11]	*-kināti*[12]
3 m	*-šun(u)*[5]	*-šunūši(m)*[13]	*-šunūti*[14]
3 f	*-šin(a)*[5]	*-šināši(m)*[15]	*-šināti*[16]

Notes: **1**. After nouns in the nom. or acc. sg.: *bēlī* "my lord". **2**. After nouns in the gen. the pron. suffix of the 1 sg. is *-ya*, e.g. *bēlī-ya* "of my lord" (in OAkk *bēlī*). After a long *u*, sometimes also after a long *a* (cf. § 13b) usually *a*, e.g. *mārū-a* "my sons" (rarely *mārū-ya*; in Mari on the other hand only *-ya: ālānū-ya* "my cities"; *tappû-ya* "my colleagues"); *qātā-a* "my hands", often *qātā-ya*. **3.** Also ventive ending (cf. § 58), only after endingless forms. **4.** After the pl. and dual forms of the 2nd and 3rd pers. After the ending *-ī* of the 2 sg. f. only *-m* (§ 58c). **4a.** OA beside *-ni*, e.g. *gimilī* "treat me kindly" (cf. § 87c). **5.** Vowelless forms are usually poetic. After a preceding short *-a* bisyllabic suffixes in OA are shortened, e.g. *ṭuppaknu* "your (pl.) tablet", *libbašnu* "your (pl.) heart" (cf. § 42d). In OAkk the suffixes of the 3rd person are *-śu, -śum, -śunu*, etc. **6.** Forms without final vowel are rare (only in the old language). **7.** Later also *-nu, -na*. **8.** In Mari *-nêšim* and *-nêti*; in OA *-niāti* is also dat. (in Bab. only acc.). Later *-nâši, -nâti*. **9.** OA *kunūti*, i.e., like the Bab. acc. suffix. **10.** OA *-kunu*, i.e., acc. suffix like the gen. suffix. **11.** OA *-kināti*. **12.** OA *-kina*. **13.** OA *-šunūti*. **14.** OA *-šunu*. **15.** OA *-šināti*. **16.** OA *-šina*.

c. Independent Possessive Pronouns 27

In the older language beside the pronominal suffix of the gen., independent pronouns were used to express the possessive relationship. They continue to be productive in OB and OA. a

b

	With masculine nouns	With feminine nouns
sg. 1	*yāʾum* "my"	*yattu*^{m}*/n* "my"
2	*kûm* (Ass. *kuāʾum*) "your"	*kattum* (Ass. *kuātum*) "your"
3	*šûm* (Ass. *šuāʾum*) "his/her/its"	*šattum, šuttum* (Ass. *šuātum*) "his/her/its"
pl. 1	*nûm* (Ass. *niāʾum*) "our"	*nuttum, niāʾtum* "our"
2	*kunûm* "your (pl.)"	(Ass. *kunūtum*) "your (pl.)"
3	*šunûm* "their"	(Ass. *šunūtum*) "their"

The pl. is formed with adjectival endings, e.g. *yāʾūtu*^{m}*/n*, *yāʾuttum* (m. pl.) "my", *yātu*^{m}*/n* (f. pl.) "my", etc., (for nunation cf.§ 29b); OA *ku(w)āʾūtum* (m. pl.) "your".

c The independent pronoun is employed either attributively, e.g. *šuāʾum bīssu* "his house", or predicatively, e.g. *bītum šū yāʾum* "that house is mine", i.e., "belongs to me". In OA it is also attested in the stative: *yât* "is mine" (f. sg.), "are mine" (f. pl.), *šūrūtum yāʾū* "black textiles are mine" (m. pl.), i.e., "I have black textiles".

d With the stem *attu-* the pron. suffixes form neologisms like *attūʾa* "mine", *attūka* "your", etc. Such neologisms later replaced the indep. poss. pronoun in Bab., e.g. *bītu attūnu* (§ 26c, sub 7) = *bīt-ni* "our house".

Note: NA *ikkû* "your (sg)", *ikkanû* "your (pl.)", *iššanû* "their" (unclear neologisms).

28 2. Reflexive Pronouns

The lack of a true reflexive pronoun "(him/her/it)self" in Akkadian is compensated for in parOt by the use of the noun *ramānum*, in Ass. *ramunum* (§ 5b, Ass. vowel harmony), NA also *ramannu*, less often through *pagrum* "body" or *napištum* "life"; cf. *ana ramānīya* "for myself", *pagarka uṣur* "protect yourself". Reflexive verbal ideas are expressed by means of special roots or stems (§ 62).

3. Demonstrative Pronouns 29

The following are employed for the demonstrative pronoun "this": a

(a) *anniu(m)*, later *annû*[46], f. *annītu(m)*, m. pl. older *anniūtu(m)*, later *annûtu(m)*, fem. older *anniātu(m)*, later *annâtu(m)*. These forms inflect like adjectives (cf. § 38g), e.g. *ṭuppī anniam* (acc.) "this tablet of mine". The f. *annītu(m)* is used independently in a neuter sense, e.g. *aššum annītim* "for this cause; therefore", *annītam* "this".

Note: In place of mimation OB (in Mari as well) often employs nunation (*annûtun, anniātun)*, which in Akkadian — just as in the independent possessive pronoun of the first pers. sg. (*yattun,* cf. § 27b) — has a determining function.[47] b

(b) *agâ* "this" (indeclinable), f. *agâtu*, appears only in later texts, e.g. *ūmu agâ* "today". In the plural it is expanded with *annû:* m. *agannûtu,* f. *agannâ/êtu*, e.g. *dibbī agannûti* "these words". Also combined with the anaphoric pronoun *šū* (§ 25a): *agāšû* "this one (m.)", f. *agāšiya*, m. pl. *agāšunu.* c

Various adjectival forms, depending on the dialect, are used for "that (one)" : d

(a) Bab. *ullû(m)*, f. *ullītu(m),* etc. — e.g. *ana mātim ullītim* "into that land".

(b) Ass. *ammiu(m)*, f. *ammītu(m)*, etc. — e.g. *ša šēpē ammâti* "on the far bank".

Note: For the adverbs of place *ullīkīʾam* "there", etc., see § 90a.

4. The Determinative Pronoun 30

ša (indeclinable) "the one of ..." serves as a determinative pronoun for all genders, e.g. *ša ḫuṭāri* "the (man) of the staff" = "staff-bearer"; neuter *ša paṭārim* "the (something) to loose". It is often employed as a circumlocution for the geni- a tive (§ 104): *šarrum ša mātim* "the king, the one of the land" = "the king of the land" (= *šar mātim).* In the first instance the emphasis rests on "king", in the second on "the land". Like English "who", "which", or "that", the determinative pronoun *ša* serves as a connecting and introductory word for the relative clause (cf. § 114).

b Actually *ša* is acc. sg. in form. In the OAkk texts (e.g., in the obelisk of Maništusu) it is still inflected: *šu, ši, ša.* The f. sg. was originally *šat*, the m. pl. *šūt*, f. pl. *šāt*. The f. sg. is frequently found in OA names like *Šat-Ištar* "the (woman) of Ištar" and in fossilized expressions: *šat mūši (urri)* "the (time) of night (or of first light)" = "nighttime (or daybreak)". (*šat urri* designates the third watch of the night, just before dawn). The pl. form *šūt* is found in expressions like *šūt rēši* "the (men) of the head" = "courtiers".

31 **5. Interrogative Pronouns**

a 1. Substantival: *mannu(m)* "who?", *manni(m)* "whose?", *ana manni(m)* "to whom?", *manna(m)* (acc.) "whom?"; *mīnu(m)* "what?", *ana mīni(m)* (also *ammīnim)* "why?", *mīna(m)* "what? (acc.)" — In addition, with final vowels lengthened by virtue of interrogatory stress (§ 24d) *minû(m), minî(m), minâ(m).* In OAkk *man*, cf. personal name *Man-ištu-šu* "who (can contend) with him?"; also with assimilation: *Ma(b)-balum-Dagan* (personal name) "who (can be) without Dagan?"

b 2. Adjectival: *ayyu(m)* (often spelled *a-a-um)* "which?", f. *ayyītu(m),* m. pl. *ayyūtu(m)*, f. pl. *ayyātu(m)* (cf. § 39e): *ayyu(m) ilu(m)* "which god?", or predicatively *ayyūtu ḫuršānū* "which are the mountains?" In OA the f. sg. is used in the neuter sense: *ana ayyītim* (spelled *a-e-tim*) "why?"

6. Indefinite Pronouns 32

Indefinite pronouns are formed from the interrogative pronouns. a

The following are formed from *mannu(m)* (§ 31a): (1) *manman* (arising from reduplication) more frequently with assimilation *mamman* (already in OB) "whoever", "anyone at all" (indeclinable, cf. OA *bīt mamman* "in anyone's house"); (2) *mamma,* originating from **manma*, *-ma* suffixed to *man* (cf. § 96); (3) *manāma, manamma*, with reversal of the components from *mammāna*. b

Others were formed from *mīnu(m)* (§ 31a): *mimma* from **min-ma* "whatever", "anything at all", "everything"; cf. *mimma annî(m)* (in gen.) "whatever of this" = "all of this", and *mimma anniam* (appositionally) "all this" (acc., cf. § 29a); likewise with a substantive, cf. OA *mimma ṣubātū* (appositionally) "all textiles", *mimma luqūtīya* "all my wares"; with direct suffixation *mimmû-ya* "my something" = "anything that is mine", declined: *mimmû-šu* (nom.), *mimmâ-šu* (acc. cf. § 42g); *mimma šumšu* (indeclinable) "whatever its name" = "anything whatsoever". c

Note: In Mari and OA *šumšu/a* after nouns stands as a kind of indefinite pronoun (literally, "whatever his/her/its name is"), e.g. *awīlūtum šumša* "anyone at all", *šīmam šumšu* "at any price at all".[48]

Still others were formed from *ayyum*: *ayyumma* "any, anyone"; f. *ayyītumma,* etc., e.g. *ilu(m) ayyumma* "any god at all". d

With negations the indefinite pronouns correspond to English "no one", etc.: *ana mamman lā tanaddin* "you may not give it to anyone" = "you may give it to no one". e

33
7. Generalizing Relatives

Among others, the following serve as generalizing relatives (cf. also § 114d sub 2): (1) (only late) the interrog. pron. *mannu* (§ 31a) in the sense of "whoever"; *mannu ša itabbalu* (NA) "whoever takes away"; (2) the indef. pron. *mimma* (§ 32c) "whatever", e.g. *mimma ša ēteppušu* "whatever I have done"; (3) *mala* (Bab.) = *ammar* (Ass.) "as much as" (cf. § 88c).

34
8. Words Expressing Totality

The words expressing totality (German *Zahlpronomina*) "all", "every" and "each" are usually (§ 32c) expressed by substantives that mean "totality", "completeness", "inclusiveness", "entirety", etc. (cf. § 102c): *gimru(m), gabbu, kalû(m), kullatu(m), napḫaru(m), seḫertu(m)*, e.g. *gimir alāni* "all cities", *ṣābum kalûšu* "the whole army".

Note: "Of every/any kind", "every" is expressed by *kalâma*, which is often inflected like a noun: *kalâmu/i/e/a*.

B. Nouns (§§ 35-46)

35
1. Roots

a In describing the formation of the Akkadian noun we distinguish two types of roots:

1. The nominal root, which is encountered in the original, primary substantives (the so-called "concrete nouns"), and is characterized by a fixed vowel pattern within the root, e.g. *abum* "father", *kalbum* "dog";

2. The verbal root, which is encountered in verbs and in substantives derived from these (deverbal). Each verbal root has either a short or a long root vowel (cf. § 1b).

According to the number of consonants, we distinguish two-, three- and four-radical roots (bi-, tri-, and quadriliteral roots). **b**

The boundary line between the Akkadian noun and verb is indistinct, since every noun can be conjugated in the stative, and the verbs possess nominal forms (participle, infinitive, verbal adj.) (cf. § 61). The adjective, which on the basis of external appearance is assigned to the noun class, belongs — according to its origin — to the verb. **c**

2. The Most Important Noun Forms **36**

The Semitic languages have formed from their roots a number of noun forms, which are sometimes distinguished by their vowel patterns and sometimes by their root augments. We can only consider here the most important cases of formation-types that in Akkadian constitute semantic classes.[49] Only the deverbal substantives and adjectives form semantic classes; semantic classes are not discernible among original, non-deverbal "concrete nouns". Although outwardly (vowel pattern, etc.) some nouns may resemble the formations of the first group, *kalbum* (§ 35a), for example, only appears to belong to the deverbal nominal form *pars(um)* (cf. § 36c), since there is no primitive verbal root **klb*. On the other hand, *aklum* "bread" (nominal form *pars)* is derived from the verbal root *ʾkl* "to eat". **a**

a. Biconsonantal Nominal Roots. **b**

The nominal forms from uni- and biconsonantal roots, such as *abum* "father", *ummum* "mother", *ilum* "god", *šarrum* "king", etc., which for the most part represent original concrete nouns with strong roots, will not be discussed here.

The biconsonantal nominal forms derived from verbal roots often belong to verbs with initial *w(a)-* (§ 80, abbrev. I *w*) that have dropped the root augment *wa-*, e.g.:

pist[50]*:* *šiptum* (**wšp)* "incantation"
pust: *šubtum* (**wšb)* "dwelling"
pis: *līdu* (**wld)* "child"

b. Nominal Forms from Triconsonantal Roots.

1' Nominal Forms without Alteration of the Radicals.

c *a) with short vowels.*

1. *pars: aklum* "bread"; Ass. *malkum* "advice" (Bab. *milkum*); *kalbatum* "bitch" (f. form, cf. § 37c).

2. *pirs: riḫṣum* "inundation"; *riḫiṣtum* (f. form, cf. § 37e) "inundation".

3. *purs: dumqum* "that which is good" (abstract from the adj.); *lubšum* "garment", *lubuštum* "garment" (§ 37e); Ass. *kuṣʾum* "cold" (Bab. *kūṣum*, cf. § 14c).

4. *paras: nakarum* (§ 7b) "hostile"; *rapšum* (contracted from **rápašum*, cf. § 7a) "broad", *rapaštum* "broad" (f. adj.).

5. *paris: laberum* (§ 7b) "old, aged"; *damqum* (contracted from **damiqum*, cf. § 7a*)* "good"; *damiqtum* (f.) "that which is good" (substantivized adj.).

6. *parus: lemnum* (Ass. *lamnum*; contracted from **lamunum)* "evil"; *lemuttum* (f., Ass. *lamuttum*) "that which is evil" (subst. adj.); the ordinal numbers also belong to this class: *ḫamšum*, f. *ḫamuštum* "fifth" (cf. § 48b).

7. *piras: zikarum* (§ 7b) "man", also *zikrum* (§ 7a).

d *b) with a long vowel.*

8. *parās*: (infinitives of the G-stem) *dabābu* "accusation" (substantivized).

9. *pirās*: *kišādum* "neck" (concrete noun).

10. *purās*: *ṣuḫāru* "small one; servant", *rubûm* < *rubāʾum* "great one; prince" (substantivized adj.).

11. *parīs: kanīkum* "sealed document" (substantivized verbal adj.).

12. *parūs*: *emūqum* (§ 6a) "strength".

13. *purūs*: *lubūšum* "attire".

14. *pāris*: (participles of the G-stem) *kāšidum* "conqueror" (substantivized adj.).

2' Nominal Forms with Doubling of a Radical.

a) With Doubling of the Second Radical. e

15. *parras:* (intensified adjectives) *qarradum* "very strong", f. *qarrattum* (§ 15a).

16. *parris: zabbilum* "porter"; *dabbibum* "slanderer"; *dabbibtum* (f.) "female slanderer".

17. *purrus* (Ass. *parrus*): α) (verbal adj. of D-stem with intensified meaning) *burrumum* "very colorful", f. *burrumtum.* β) (persons with bodily defects) *kubburum* "obese". γ) (D-stem inf.) *lummudum* "to instruct" (cf. on this § 64d).

18. *parrās:* (occupational designations) *šarrāqum* "thief", *errēšum* (§ 5a) "plowman", *kaššāpum* "sorcerer", *kaššaptum* (f.) "witch"; *dayyānum*[51] "judge".

19. *parrūs*: *šakkūrum* "drunken".

b) With Doubling of the Third Radical. f

20. *parass: agammum* "swamp", *eleppum* "ship" (concrete nouns).

21. *paruss:* (intensive adj. with numinous content) *namurrum* "gleaming awesomely"; also substantivized f. *rašubbatu* "awesomeness".

22. *piriss*: *gimillum* "kind deed".

23. *puruss*: *ḫubullum* “debt”.

3’ Nominal Forms with Preformatives.

g ***a) With aleph (ʾ).***

24. *apras*: (very rare) *arbaʾum* “four”.

25. *ipris*: *ikribum* “prayer”, *ipṭerum* “ransom money”.

h ***b) With m-.***

26. *mapr*^{a}*/ās:* (among other things, forms nouns of place) *makn*^{a}*/ākum* “sealed container”; *maškanum* “place”, *maškānum* “storehouse”; *na-* instead of *ma-* before roots containing a labial (§ 18a)*:* *napḫarum* “total”, *nērebtum* (§ 6a) “entrance”.

27. *mapris*:. *mēt*^{i}*/equm* “exit”, *nešmû* “(faculty of) hearing” (cf. above sub 26); *melqētum* (f., Ass. *malqētu*) “(a kind of tax)”.

28. *mupr*^{a}*/ās*: *muṣlālum* “noon, siesta time”.

Note: The prefix *mu-,* unlike *ma-* (§ 18a), remains unchanged before labials (cf. above sub 26): *mušpalum* “depth”: an exception is *nubattum* (from *biātum* “to spend the night”*)* “evening”. With weak verbs certain phonetic changes occur, such as *mūšabum* (**wšb)* from **muwšabum* .

***c. With* na- *(not the result of dissimilation from* ma-).**

29. *naprus*: (N stem infinitives) *nalbubum* “to be(come) wild” (§ 66c).

i ***d. With* š- *(Š- stem, cf. § 65).***

30. *šapras*: *šapšaqum* “constriction, oppression, anxiety”.

31. *šaprus*: *šalbubu* “wild”; *šaḫluqtum* (f. form) “loss, ruin”.

32. *šuprus* (Ass. *šaprus*): (inf. and verbal adj. of the Š-stem) *šuršudum* “firmly grounded, made firm”; intensive forms like *šurbûm* “huge, very large”.

e. *With* ta-. j

33. *tapras:* (Nouns of place) *tarbaṣum* "courtyard".

34. *taprās:* (reciprocal sense) *tāḫāzum* "battle, combat" (from **taʾḫāzum*, root **ʾḫz*, i.e., "seizing one another"), *tamḫārum* "battle encounter".

35. *taprīs:* (action nouns of the D-stem) *taklīmum* "offering", *tamšīlum* "copy, replica".

36. *taprus*: f. form *tamgurtum* "mutual agreement" (reciprocal sense); *tapšuḫtum* "rest", *tērubtum* "entrance"; OA *taššītum* (**nšī*) "transporting".

4' Nominal Forms with Infixed -*t*- . k

37. *pitrās: gitmālum* "complete, perfect".

38. *pitrus*: (inf. of G-stem) *mitḫuṣum* "battle".

5' Nominal Forms with Sufformatives. l

39. *purussāʾ* (action nouns or juristic concepts): *purussûm* (suff. *-ûm* from *-āʾum*) "decision, verdict", *rugummûm* "charge, accusation", *uzubbûm* "divorce payment, divorce settlement", OA *ḫuluqqāʾum* "lost wares".

40. *-ûm*: (from *-īum*): forms ethnica like *Aššurûm* < *Aššurīum*, f. *Aššurītum* "Assyrian".

41. *-ūtum*: (Ass. *-uttum*): forms abstracts (grammatically f.)[52]: *šarrūtum* "kingship", *Ellilūtum* "Enlil-ship, authority of Enlil", *šībūtum* (Ass. *šībuttum*) "testimony", OA *ebaruttum* "friendship".

42. *-ānum:* (to designate actors in a single incident) *nādinānum* "the seller (in a particular transaction)", *šarrāqānum* "thief (in a particular theft)" vs. *šarrāqum* "thief" (cf. above in section e 18).

43. *-ān* + *-ī*: *bābānû* "exterior (adj.)", *ḫurāṣānītu* (f.) "goldfinch".

44. *-āyum* (later *-āya*) forms ethnica: *Eluḫatāyum* "man from Eluḫat", later *Ṣidunnāya* "Sidonian".

Note: Perhaps the NA nisbe (spelled A + A) is to be pronounced *-iyu* rather than the traditional *-āya*, since the f. counterpart ends in *-ītu* (K. Deller).

m Numerous words in Akkadian are of Sumerian origin, e.g. *ṭuppu(m)* "tablet" from Sum. d u b. Many Sumerian loan words are formed with the Sum. genitive ending - a k, e.g. *išš(i)akkum*[53] "city ruler". There are also compounds that were loaned from Sum., e.g. *kisalluḫum* "purifier of the temple court" (from k i s a l "court" and l u ḫ "to purify"); *ekallum* "palace" (from é "house" and g a l "large").

37 **3. Gender**

a Nouns distinguish masculine and feminine genders.

b The f. sg. is used for the substantival neuter of the adjective: *lemuttum* "evil" (noun), *ṭābtum* "that which is good", *kittum* "truth" (**kīntum)*.

c The m. is represented by the bare stem: *šarr-um* (*-u* case ending, § 39b: *-m* mimation, § 18c) "king", *mār-um* (from *marʾum,* cf. § 14b) "son", *ell-um* "pure". The f. adds a *t* to the end of the stem: *mār-t-um* "daughter". If the stem ends in a doubled consonant or is of the form *pars* (§ 36c), *-at-* is added instead of *-t-,* which in Bab. becomes *-et-* after *e-* containing syllables (§ 5a), *šarr-at-um* "queen", *ell-et-um*" (Ass. *ell-ut-um*, § 5b*)* "pure (female), *kalb-at-um* "bitch", OA *merʾ-ut-um* "daughter".[54]

d Elided short vowels (§ 7a) reappear in f. sg.: *šakin-tu* (f. of *šakn-u* < **šakin-u)* "high-ranking female administrator".

e Monosyllabic triconsonantal stems of *pirs* and *purs* types are enlarged internally, when the external f. ending is added, by the insertion of a short homophonous vowel (cf. §§ 11a and 36c): *riḫṣum* "inundation", f. *riḫiṣ-t-um*; *pulḫum* "fear", f. *puluḫ-t-um.*

Stems with final *-n,* show assimilation of *-nt-* to *-tt-* (§ 16b): *lemuttum,* m. *lemnum* "evil" from **lamunum* (§ 7a). Yet note one exception: *šakintu* (§ 37d) beside NA *šakittu.* **f**

In the later stages of the language (MB and MA and later) a sibilant before *t* dissimilates to *l* (§ 28b): *rapaltu* < *rapaštu,* m. *rapšu* "wide" from **rap(a)šu*; this secondary *lt* sequence then becomes *ss* in NA (§ 15c): *šalassu* (NA f.) "three", < MB *šalaltu* < OB *šalaštum*; *mazzassu* (NA) < MB *mazzaltu*, OB *mazzaztum* "position". **g**

dt becomes *tt*: *maʾadu* "much", f. *maʾattu* (NA rarely *maʾassu*, § 15c). **h**

Many words are f. in gender without the external f. ending *-t-:* **i**

(a) natural (i.e. biological) feminines like *ummum* "mother", *atānum* "jenny",

(b) parts of the body occurring in pairs: *īnum* "eye", *uznum* "ear", even *rēšum* "head" *lišānum* "tongue",

(c) substantives like *ḫarrānum* "road", *ḫaṭṭum* "staff", *eleppum* "ship", *ereqqum* "wagon", OA *naruqqum* "sack", *šuqlum* "container".

Several are of common gender (§ 38 l): *ekallum* "palace", *gerrum* "road, journey".

4. Number **38**

Nouns distinguish three numbers: singular, plural and dual. **a**

The dual (in the declined state rare already in OB) is employed with parts of the body that occur in pairs and with sev- **b** eral other words considered to be in the same category: *idān* "(two) hands", *īnān* "(two) eyes", *emūqān* "strength of arms".

c In older Akkadian and OA, esp. after the numeral "two", the dual is still widely employed (even with adjectives, cf. § 101c): *2 nēpešān* "two ingots", *2 naruqqēn* (acc.) "two sacks"; *2 šūrēn damqēn* (acc.) "two good black stuffs (cloths)", *šēwirān anniān* (OAkk) "these two rings/bracelets".

d In the pl., masc. and fem., substantives and adjectives are differently declined. Cf. Paradigms I-IV.

I. SUBSTANTIVES

e The pl. of m. substantives has the following endings:

1. *-ū,* e.g. *šarrum* "king", pl. *šarrū.*

2. *-ānu*[55], attested already in OB (esp. Mari) and OA,[56] e.g. *šarrānu* "kings" (in the sense of "individual kings"), in contrast to *šarrū* "the kings" (as a group); *ālānu* (OA and Mari) "individual cities", versus *ālū* "the cities"; *ilānu* "the (chief) deities", versus *ilū* "gods" (as a pantheon).

f Fem. substantives add a pl. ending *-ātu(m)* to the bare stem: sg. *šarratu(m)* "queen", pl. *šarrātu(m)*; Bab. *-ētu(m)* following an *e* sound (§ 5a): *bēlētu(m)* "ladies, mistresses" (Ass. *bēlātum*). In MB and MA and later the mimation is dropped (cf. § 18c).

g The biradical substantives *abu(m)* "father", *aḫu(m)* "brother", and *iṣu(m)* "tree" have consonantal doubling in the plural: *abbū, aḫḫū, iṣṣū.*

h Several substantives are always plural in form without possessing a true plural sense in English (so-called p l u r a l e t a n t u m): *mû* (<*māʾū*), SB *māwū* (< *māmū*) "water"; *šamû* (< *šamāʾū*), SB *šamāwū* (< *šamāmū*) "heaven, sky"; OA *dašʾū* (Bab. *dīšum*) "(season of) spring"; *aršātum* "barley".

Irregular f. pl. formations: *alkakātum* (from *alaktum*) "way, i
road"; *asītātu* (NA) beside *asayātu* from Ass. *asītu* "tower". Cf. also OA plurals like *aḫuʾātum* from *aḫātum* "sister", *meruʾātum* (or *meruwātum)* from *merʾutum* (cf. § 37c) "daughter", *luquātum* from *luqūtum* "ware". An *n* that in the singular has assimilated (cf. § 37f) will reappear in the plural: *šattum* (< **šantum)* "year", plural *šanātum.*

Many words exhibit the feminine ending only in plural, and j
are not consistently treated as feminine grammatically: *gerrum* (§ 37i) "road", pl. *gerrētum*; *ekallum* "palace", pl. *ekallātum*; further, designations of persons who function alone, e.g. *ḫazannum* "mayor", pl. *ḫazannātu* (MB, SB). Several words employ either m. or f. endings in plural: *nasīku(m)* "prince", pl. *nasīkānu, nasīkātu.*

II. ADJECTIVES

The adjectives of feminine gender form plurals like the k
feminine substantives. Masc. adjectives, on the other hand, instead of the *ā* (or *ē*) of the fem., employ an *ū: malkātu(m) dannātu(m)* "powerful princesses"; *malkū dannūtu(m)* "powerful princes".

Note: Substantivized adjectives and participles form the plural some- l
times adjectivally, sometimes substantivally, cf. *šaknūtu* "governors" (sg. *šaknu),* literally "installed ones" (§ 61c); but *mundaḫṣī/ē* (beginning in MB, older *muntaḫṣum* from **mḫṣ* "to smite") "warriors" (Gt participle, § 67d).

5. The Declined State and Declension 39

A noun on which no genitive is dependent stands in the a
declined state. In its inflexion it distinguishes three cases: nominative, genitive and accusative. In the earlier stages of the language two further cases are known: the locative-ad-

verbial in *-u(m)* (§44) and the terminative-adverbial in *-iš* (§45). For further adverbial endings cf. §90.

b In the older language (OB, OA) the nom. sg. has the ending *-um*, gen. sg. *-im*, acc. sg. *-am* (regardless of whether m. or f., subst. or adj.). Later (MB, MA) the final *m* (so-called "mimation") is lost (§18c). Sometimes the mimation is lacking even in the earlier stages, esp. in personal names, e.g. *Abu-(wa)qar* (OA) "father is dear". In NB and NA, moreover, the three cases are no longer strictly distinguished. In particular, the acc. is frequently replaced by the nom. In LB utter arbitrariness often reigns. In these later periods older forms will often occur, partly as deliberate archaisms (§2d).

c Proper names often appear as indeclinable nominatives (as early as OB), e.g. ^{d}*Zarpanītum bēltīya* (Code of Hammurapi) "of my lady Zarpanitum" (gen.); *mār Tarībum* "the son of Taribum" (vs. *Subartum, -tim, -tam* "(land of) Subartu"). Divine names sometimes stand in the absolute state (§43, originally probably only a vocative), e.g. ^{d}*Šamaš* "(the sungod) Šamaš", but ^{d}*šamšum* "sun"; ^{d}*Bēl* "(the god) Bel", but *bēlum* "lord" (cf. also §43d).

d The dual distinguishes only two cases, which are formed with the endings *-ān* in the nom., and (Bab.) *-īn* or (Ass.) *-ēn* (both from **-ayn*) in the gen./acc., e.g. m.: *šēpān* (nom.), *šēp*^{ī}*/ēn* (gen./acc.) "two feet", f. *šaptān* "two lips" (sg. *šaptum* "lip"), *šapt*^{ī}*/ēn*. The final *-n* is dropped from MB and SB on. In the phonetic spelling of "2", *š*^{i}*/enā*, the final *-n* is regularly missing.

The plurals, like the duals, have only two case forms: e

	Subst. m.	adj. m.	adj. f.
nom.	*-ū, -ānu*[57]	*-ūtu(m)*	*-ā/ētu(m)*
gen./acc.	*-ī,* (Ass.) *-ē, -āni*[1]	*-ūti(m)*	*-ā/ēti(m)*

For f. pl. *-ēt*^{u}*/i(m)* instead of *-āt*^{u}*/i(m)* cf. § 38f.

Note: In the Mari texts one encounters a special acc. form for a collective pl. f. — the ending *-ātam,*[58] e.g. *ummanātam* "troops". Anything like this in the later texts would have to be labeled incorrect.

6. Nouns with a Weak Third Radical 40

If the noun stem ends in a vowel, the two vowels that are juxtaposed when a case ending is added contract according to the rules of § 9a (except for *i-a)* — this had already begun in OB: *rabûm* "large" beside *rabium*, gen. *rabîm*, acc. *rabiam* (normal form in OB) becomes *rabâ(m)*; *rubāʾum* "prince" becomes *rubû(m), rubāʾim* (gen.) becomes *rubê(m), *šurbuʾum* "exalted" becomes *šurbû(m)*; **šadu-im*[59] (gen.) "of the mountain" becomes *šadî(m).* Accordingly, the resulting sg. endings are: *-û(m)* (nom.), *-â(m)* (acc.), *-î(m)* (gen.), and *-ê(m),* a contraction of *ā-i* (cf. also § 9b). a

In the pl. *rubāʾū* becomes *rubû*, gen. *rubāʾī* becomes *rubê.* Short final stem vowels often contract with the long vowels of the plural endings, esp. in the later stages of the language: *rabûtu(m)* from *rabiūtum,* f. *rabâtu(m)* from *rabiātum.* b

In the sg., f. nouns and adjectives have a long vowel before the ending *-t: rabītum* "large"; *rubātum* "female ruler"; *šurbūtum* "exalted". The declension offers no irregularities. Cf. Parad. V-VI. c

Uncontracted forms (§ 9b) occur in OAkk, and partly in OB and in Ass.: *rubāʾum*, later *rubû*; *warkium* "later", Ass. *urkium* (§ 12a) becomes *arkû*; *šamāʾī* "of the sky", later *šamê.* d

41 7. The Construct State

a The genitive always follows its governing noun. The latter then stands in the construct state (combinatory form). This forms with the following genitive a unit of accentuation (§ 24b). The construct before the dependent gen. shows no distinction in form for the different cases (i.e., it exhibits the same form for the nom., acc., and gen.), e.g. *bīt awīlim* is either "the house of a citizen" (nom. and acc.) or "of the house of a citizen" (gen.).

b In the construct the mimation together with the preceding short vowel is dropped, e.g. m. *bēl* is constr., for *bēl-um* "lord"; f. *šarrat* and *ellet* are constr. forms of *šarrat-um* "queen" and *ellet-um* "pure (f.)". The same rule holds for *-n* in the dual (§ 39d); *šēpā, šēpī/ē* are constr. forms of *šēpān* and *šēpī/ēn* "two feet". The construct forms of *šumum* "name" and *qātum* "hand" in OA end in *-i: šumi, qāti* (the latter attested also in OB).

c *Note*: In the older stages of the language (OAkk and in part in OA) the gen. of the construct ends in *-i*.[60] OAkk *in bīti* PN "in the house of PN"; in OA attested always in combination: *ina šamši* or *iššamši* "on the day on which" (cf. § 88b). Yet cf. OA *iqqabli ḫarrānim* "in the course of the business trip" beside *iqqabal ḫarrānim*. OA *kalûm* "everything" inflects triptotically in the construct[61]: *kalu merʾēya* "all my sons", gen. *ša kali kaspim* "for the money, acc. *kala awâtīni* "all our affairs" (§ 42g).

d Monosyllabic stems with final doubled consonant add an epenthetic vowel *-i* in the construct, e.g. *ṭuppi*, the construct of *ṭuppum* "tablet". Rarely, forms of the above type lack the doubling in the final cons.: *šarrum* "king", construct *šar kiššatim* "king of everything (of the universe)". If the stem is bi- or polysyllabic, the final doubled consonant is regularly simplified: *kunuk* (from *kunukkum*) “seal”; *naruq* (from *naruqqum)* “sack” (OA).

Monosyllabic forms of the types *pars, pirs, purs* (§ 36c) are normally enlarged to two syllables in the construct through the insertion of an epenthetic vowel: (cf.§ 11a and 37e): *kalbum* “dog”, construct *kalab*; *šiprum* “work”, construct *šipir*; *šulmum* “well-being”, construct *šulum* (Ass. *šipar, šulam).* Regarding the epenthetic vowel *a* inserted before *l, r, m* and *n* in OA cf. § 11b. **e**

Elided vowels (§ 7a and 37d) reappear in the construct: *šaknum* “deputy” from **šakinum*, construct *šakin* . **f**

Fem. nouns ending in *-t* mostly form their constructs with the external helping vowel *-i*: *seḫerti mātim* “the circumference of the land”; *ukulti emārī* (OA) “fodder for asses”. Still, also (usually in monosyllabic stems; with polysyllabic ones only in proper names and in poetry) with *-at*/*-et* (§ 37c), e.g. *napiš-t-um* “life”, has a construct *napš-at* beside *napišti*; *epiš-t-um* “work”, construct *epš-et* beside *epišti*; *šīm-t-um* “fate”, construct *šīm-at* beside *šīmti.* **g**

The original vowel of the final syllable of nouns having a weak third radical reappears in the construct: *bāni,* “builder of”, construct state of participle *bānium, bānû(m)*; *tappa* “colleague”, construct of *tappāʾum*, later *tappû(m).* A later way of handling these forms is to completely drop the third radical and its vowel: *bān* beside *bāni*, *aššu kas puriddī* (SB) “in order to bind the feet”. **h**

The plural ending *-ū* is preserved in the construct. The plural endings *-ūtu(m)* (m. adj.) and *-ā/ētu(m)* (f.) appear in the construct as *-ūt* and *-ā/ēt*; *-ūt* can be replaced by the construct **i** of the sg. (§ 108b); cf. *āšib parakki* (SB) "those who sit upon the throne", beside *āšibūt parakki*.

42 8. Nouns with Suffixes

a Pronominal suffixes too are added to the construct of the noun, but completely fuse with it to form a single word. In the case of gen. nouns in the construct with pron. suffixes, the gen. *-i* always occurs between the noun and the suffix and is lengthened by virtue of the accent shift accompanying the addition of pron. suffixes (cf. § 24b); hence, *bēlī-šu* "of his lord". Nom. and acc. employ the same forms: *bēl-šu* "his lord", *bēlī* "my lord" (for exceptions, cf. § 42g).

Note: A subst. with a following pron. suffix need not be definite, e.g. *īn-šu* "one of his (two) eyes".

b The forms of the pron. suffix (see § 26b). The suffix of the 1 sg. *-ī* is added to the declined state, e.g. *napišt-ī* "my life", but also (only poetic) *napšat-ka* beside normal *napišta-ka*; *qīšt-ī* "my gift", but *qīšta-ka*. Note that *-ya* is retained only after vowels: *bēlī-ya* "of my lord", *uznā-ya* (§ 26c under 2) "my (two) ears", *mārū-ya* "my children". According to § 13b, *y* is often dropped: *uznāʾa, mārūʾa*.

c *š* in pron. suffixes of the 3rd pers. becomes *s*, when it follows dentals or sibilants (§ 20c). This also occurs with f. forms ending in *-t: šallas-su* "his booty" from *šallat-šu*; *bēlūs-su* "his lordship" from **bēlūt-šu*; *awās-sa* "her word" from **awāt-ša*.

d The vowel *a* is added to the (unsimplified) double consonants as a helping vowel: *libba-šu* "his heart". In Ass. the "Ass. vowel harmony" affects this connecting vowel when the pron. suffix is monosyllabic: *líbbu-šu*, but not when the pron. suffix is bisyllabic, since there occurs a shift in the placement of word stress,[62] thus *libbá-š(u)nu* "their heart(s)" (cf. § 5b-c).

Stems of the forms *pars, pirs, purs* stand in the same relationship to the following pron. suffixes as such forms in the construct do to the following dependent nouns in the gen. case (§ 41e), e.g. *šipir-šu* "his work", Ass. *šipar-šu.* e

Monosyllabic noun stems with the f. ending *-t*, when they employ internal helping vowels, prefer *a*, e.g. *ṣibas-su* "his interest (nom./acc.)" from **ṣibat-šu* (the declined state is *ṣibtum).* But sometimes such monosyllabic feminines take an external helping vowel, in which cases again this vowel is *a*: *qīšta-ka* "your gift". This formation is regular in polysyllabic stems, e.g. *napišta-ka* (see § 42b). Compare the external *-i* in the construct before gen. according to § 41g. f

Nominal forms of roots with final weak consonants are fully declined before suffixes, i.e., they take a distinct vocalic case ending before the pron. suffix for (in addition to the gen in *-i)* nom. in *-ū* and acc. in *-ā*: g

1. stems ending in *-a*, e.g. *kalû-šu* (§ 41c), *kalî-šu, kalâ-šu* "all" (OA with vowel harmony: *kulû-šu, kilî-šu)*: *mimmû-šu* (§ 32c), *mimmâ-šu* "anything that belongs to him";

2. stems ending in *-ā:* infinitives of the G-stem with third radical weak (§ 83), e.g. *našâ-šu* (acc.) "his carrying" (OA uncontracted: *laqāʾū-šu* "his taking"), or noun forms *purussāʾum* (§ 36 l), e.g. *purussû-šu* "his decision".

3. noun forms of the type *pars, pirs, purs* with third radical weak: *ḫīṭū-šu* (w. compensatory lengthening from *ḫiṭʾum*, cf. § 14c) "his punishment", *bīšā-šu* "his possessions" (acc.), *mārā-šu* "his son" (acc.).

The forms taken by *abum* "father", *aḫum* "brother" and *emum* "father-in-law" before pronoun suffixes are normally *abū-* (nom.), *abī-* (gen.), *abā-* (acc.) (so also *aḫū-, aḫī-, aḫā-,* h etc.). In NA *aḫ-šu* "his brother" occurs beside *aḫū-šu* (nom.). With the suffix of the 1st pers. sg. the form is regularly *abī* "my father", *aḫī* "my brother", but in MB and NA also *abūʾa* and *aḫūʾa*.

i Through analogy with the m. pl. in *-ū*, the vowel before the pron. suffix in such forms as *-ūtu(m)* and *-ā/ētu(m)* is lengthened, e.g. *epšētū-a* (§ 26e, note 2) "my works", *epšētī-šu* "of his works".

43 **9. The Absolute State**

a In the singular, the absolute state resembles the 3rd pers. sg. of the stative (§ 54a). As a matter of fact, the stative (3rd pers.) and the absolute state regularly coincide in form, but in other respects differ quite sharply. In the m. the absolute state appears as the bare stem, e.g. *bēl* "lord". The fem. sg. ending is *-at*, e.g. *šanat* "a year". After an *e* in the stem the *a* in the f. ending assimilates to *e* in Bab. (§ 5a) (but not in Ass.), e.g. *bēlet* "lady", Ass. *bēlat*. In the f. pl.[63] it has the ending *-āt* (in OA), e.g. 3 *šanāt* "three years", or *-ā* (in OB, without the *-t* and indeclinable), e.g. 3 *šiqlā* "3 shekels" (to a certain extent even in OA: 4 *naruqqā* "4 sacks").

b The absolute state is often employed in certain fixed expressions, such as *zikar sinniš* "male (and) female", *ṣeḫer rabi* "small (and) great", *batiq wattur* "cheap (or) expensive" (OA), particularly with the negated infinitive: *šar lā šanān* "king without an equal" (cf. § 103d).

c Distributive expressions also stand in the absolute state, e.g. OA *ina kār kār-ma* "in every colony", OB *ana māt māt-ma* "for every land", *ina ellat ellat* "with every caravan".

Cardinal numbers (§ 47b, e) and the units of measure also stand in the absolute state, e.g. *ḫamšat šiqil kaspum* "five shekels of silver". **d**

The absolute state can be used as a vocative, e.g. *etel* "man!", *kalab* "dog!" (for *Šamaš*, etc., see § 39c). **e**

10. Adverbial Ending -*um* (Locative) **44**

The adverbial in -*um*, like the adverbial in -*iš*, (§ 45) represents an old case form, which in the earlier stages of the language (OAkk, OA) was still in active use. The ending -*um* was employed for the locative function, thereby corresponding to the gen. preceded by the prep. *ina* or *ana*. **a**

This adverbial is encountered either independently without a prepos., e.g. OA *ištēn manāʾum* "in/for one mina", or with the prepos. *ina* or *ana*, e.g. OA *ana mētum* "percent (%)". **b**

The loc.-adv. in -*um* is often construed with the following dependent gen. or pron. suffix, e.g. *qerbum Bābili* "in (the midst of) Babylon". With preceding prep., e.g. *ina libbu* (without final -*m*) *mātim* "inside the land". **c**

The final -*m* assimilates (§ 18d) before the pron. suffixes, e.g. *šaptukki* (from **šaptum-ki*) = *ina šaptī-ki* "on your (f.) lip"; *qerbuššu* = *ina qerbī-šu* "in its midst". With the suff. of 1 sg. *šēpūʾa* "at my foot" (SB) from **šēpum-ya* . **d**

Note: Attached to the inf. stem, -*um* is employed in paronomastic constructions (cf. 109d). For the loc. ending -*um* cf. § 90c. **e**

11. Adverbial Ending in -*iš* (terminative) **45**

The ending -*iš* (in Mari still independent as the preposition *iš* with the meaning of *ana*[64]) originally had a terminative, later a locative, function, e.g. *qerbiš* "in the midst". It should be considered in the light of the -*š* - in the dative forms of the **a** pers. pron. (§ 25c). Cf. the old personal name *Iliš-tikal* "trust in the god". With the inf., OA *muātiš* "for dying" (cf. also § 109f). Occasionally pleonastically with prepos., e.g. *ana dāriš* "forever".

b The adverbial in *-iš,* like the loc.-adv., sometimes occurs with dependent gen., e.g. *dāriš ūmī* "forever" (also with prep. *ana dāriš ūmī).* In poetic texts *bītiš emūtim* "in the house of the bride's family", or with pron. suffix., e.g. *šēpiš-šu* "at his foot").

c In the later stages of the language the adv. in *-iš* is often the semantic equivalent of *kīma* + gen. "like a", e.g. *abūbiš* = *kīma abūbim* "like a flood" (sometimes with *-āniš: abūbāniš).*

d The adv. *-iš* occurs very often with adjectives, e.g. *ṭābiš* "in a kindly manner, graciously", *arḫiš* "speedily", *lamniš* (OA) "badly".

e The ending *-iš* + the acc./adv. ending *-am* (§ 90a) = *-išam,* which is used principally for distributive adverbs: *(w)arḫišam* "monthly".

46 12. Comparison of Adjectives

a Comparative and superlative in Akkadian are not expressed by separate endings of the adjective, but by syntactical circumlocutions.

1. Comparative. The prep. *eli* "above, over" is used to express this: SB *ekallu eli maḫrīti naklat* "the palace was more beautiful than the previous one"; "more so than previously" is expressed *eli ša ūm pāni, eli ša pāna, eli ša maḫri,* etc.

b II. Superlative. To express this idea either adjectives with intensified meaning of the forms *purrus* (§ 36e) or *šuprus* (§ 36 i) or also special adj. with the gen. (usually in the pl.)

are employed: *Ištar šurbūt ilāni* "Ishtar, the exalted among deities" = "the highest deity"; *leʾi kal malkī* "the able of all princes" = "the most able prince"; *ašarēd kal malkī* "the pre-eminent prince".

C. Numbers (§§ 47-50)

1. Cardinal Numbers **47**

Cardinal numbers are usually expressed by numerals, leaving the pronunciation of many numbers unknown for Akkadian. **a**

The cardinal numbers 1-10 are used in the declined and absolute states (§ 43d). Both distinguish m. and f. For the grammatical construction of cardinal numbers and numbered nouns cf. § 107a/b. **b**

c

	declined st.		**absolute st.**	
	m.	f.	m.	f.
1	(*ištēnum*)	(*ištētum*)	*ištēn*	*ištiat*, later *ištēt*
2	*ši/ena*	*šitta*[2]	*ši/ena*	*šitta*
3	*šalāšum*	*šalaštum*[3]	*šalaš*	*šalāšat*
4	*erbûm*[4]	*erbettum*	*erba*[4]	*erbet*[4]
5	*ḫamšum*[5]	*ḫamištum*	*ḫamiš*	*ḫamšat*[6]
6	*šeššum*[6]	*šedištum*	?	*šeššet*[7]
7	*sebûm*	*sebettum*	*sebe*	*sebet*
8	(*samānûm*)	*samānūtu*	*samāne*[8]	(*samanat*)
9	*tišûm*	*t^{i}/ešītum*[9]	*tiše*	*tiš^{e}/it*[10]
10	*ešrum*	*ešertum*[11]	*ešer*	*ešeret*

Notes. **1.** Only OA and OB. **2.** From **šinta*. On the orig. dual *šittān* "2/3"see § 49. **3.** In later Bab. *šalaltu* (§ 20b), NA *šalassu* (§ 15c); OA *šalištum* "party of three". **4.** declined state OAkk *arbaʾum*, absolute st. OA *arba*, f. *arbet*. **5.** Also *ḫanšu, ḫaššu* (§ 18e); **6.** From **šadšum* (§ 15a). **7.** OB also *šiššet*. **8.** OA *šamāne*. **9.** Later *tiltu* (§ 20b) from **tištu*. **10.** OB also *tešīt*. **11.** OA *ešartum* "party of ten".

d Only a few of the numerals 11-19 are attested in the absolute state, e.g. 17 *sebēšer* (m.), 18 *samānēšer* (m.), *samānēšeret* (f.), 11 both *ištenšeret* and *istēn ešret* (f.).

e The numerals 20-50 are f. pl. of the absolute state in -*ā*[65]: 20 *ešrā*, 30 *šalāšā*, 40 *erbâ*, 50 *ḫanšā* (from *ḫamšā)* or *ḫaššā* (before suff.: *ḫamšat-sunu*!).

f The higher numbers partially follow the sexagesimal and partially the decimal system: 60 is *šuššu*, 100 *meʾat* (absolute st.), *mētum* (declined state), 600 *nēr* (absolute state), 1000 *lim* (absolute state), 3600 *šar* (absolute state).

g "Both" is *kilallān* or *kilallūn,* f. *kilattān* (gen.-acc. *kilattēn),* OA *kilaltān*; with suff. *kilallā-šunu* "the two of them", *akkilallē-kunu* (OA) "to/for the two of you" (cf. § 88b).

48 2. Ordinal Numbers

a The ordinal number "first" is expressed either by the cardinal number *ištēn* or by the adj. *maḫrû(m)* "former, first"; OA *pānium.*

b The ordinals 2-10 frequently have the form *parus* (§ 36c):

m.	f.	Translation
šanûm	*šanītum*	"second"
šalšum[1]	*šaluštum*[1]	"third"
rebûm	*rebūtum*	"fourth"
ḫamšum [2]	*ḫamuštum* [2]	"fifth"
šeššum [3]	(*šeduštum*[3])	"sixth"
sebûm	*sebūtum*	"seventh"
samnum [4]	*samuntum* [4]	"eighth"
tišûm	(*tišūtum)*?	"ninth"
ešrum	*ešurtum*	"tenth"

1. OA *šališum,* f. *šalištum,* OAkk *śalištum.* **2.** Also *ḫanšu, ḫaššu* (§ 18e); c
OA f. *ḫamištum.* **3.** From **šadšum* (§ 15a); OA *šadāšum,* f. *š^a/edištum.* **4.** Also *samānû, samānūtu.*

Other ordinals: *ištenšerû* "eleventh", *šinšerû* "twelfth", *šalaššerû* d
"thirteenth", *erbēšerû* "fourteenth", *ešrû* (only SB) "twentieth", *š^e/alāšû* "thirtieth".

3. Fractions 49

Fractions either take the form *paris* or *parus* or are expressed by special substantives, e.g. $^1/2$ *mišlu(m),* $^1/3$ *šalšu(m),* f. *šalištu(m),* $^2/3$ *šittān* (cf. § 47c) or *šinepâtu(m),* construct *šinepât* or *šinepu* (actually composite from *šina* "2" and *pûm* "mouth"), $^5/6$ *parasrab* (lit., "great portion"). With other fractions the denominator, which follows the numerator in absolute state, will be the f. pl. of the ordinal: $^3/4$ *šalaš rebât* (absolute state), lit., "three fourths". Plur. tantum in OA *ešrātum* "$^1/10$".

4. Multiplicatives 50

Multiplicatives are formed by adding an adverbial ending *-ī* (cf. § 90j) and the pron. suff. *-šu* "its" to the cardinal: *šal(a)šī-šu* "thrice", *ḫamšī-šu* "five times"; often preceded by prep. *adi: adi šinī-šu* "twice", *adi ešrā-šu* (OA) "ten times".

D. Verbs (§§ 51-87)

1. Conjugation and the Strong Verb (§§ 51-61)

a. Verbal Roots 51

The large majority of verbal roots is triconsonantal (the so- a
called strong verbs); several roots have four consonants, while many others consist of only two consonants (so-called "weak verbs"). To every root there belongs a short or a long root vowel (e.g., **pq^{i}d,* **kūn,* **bnī),* which appears in the pret. and imp. of the G-stem (cf. § 1b).

b By means of the various root vowels one can establish (in the triconsonantal roots) certain semantic classes of verbs. But these semantic classes can only be distinguished by the root vowels in the case of "fientic" (German *fientisch*) verbs, i.e., verbs that describe actions. They cannot be distinguished by this criterion in the case of "stative" verbs (not verbs in the stative), i.e., those that describe states or qualities and that ultimately derive from adjectives. For further discussion of the various semantic classes to which a verb may be assigned according to the quality of its root vowel, cf. § 63b.

c Within the category of fientic verbs there is furthermore a special group of denominative verbs attested principally in the D-stem (cf. § 64f).

52

b. Conjugation

a The conjugation of the Akkadian verb (pres., pret., and perf.) is achieved through the use of suffixes alone, or a combination of prefixes and suffixes. The stative (cf. Parad. XI) is formed with the help of the following endings, which in the case of the verb are suffixed to the endingless form of the 3 m. sg., or in the case of the noun (§ 43a) to the absolute state.

b

	sg.	dual	pl.
3 m	–	*-ā*	*-ū*
3 f.	*-at*	*-ā*	*-ā*
2 m	*-āta* (OA *-āti*)		*-ātunu*
2 f.	*-āti*		*-ātina*
1 c	*-āku*		*-ānu* (Ass. *-āni*)

c The stative has no ending in the 3 m. sg., resembling the absolute state of the noun (cf. § 43a); in the 3 f. sg. it has the ending *-at*. The m. pl. ends in *-ū*, the f. in *-ā*. With the other persons the pronouns of the 1st and 2nd pers. are involved, being connected to the endingless stem by the connecting vowel *-ā-*. These pronouns assume a shortened form. If the verb contains an *e*, the connecting vowel will be *-ē-* instead of *-ā-* (cf. § 5a), i.e., *-et, -ēta, -ēti, -ēku*, etc., e.g. *šeber* "is broken", *šebret, šebrēta,* etc.

Note: Beside *-ātina* OA has *-ātini*, cf. *sinnišātini* "you are women".

P r e s e n t, p r e t e r i t e and p e r f e c t (parad. XII, **d**
XIII, XIVa) are conjugated verbally, and indeed all in the same way.

Sg. 3 m.	*i-*....................	*u-*....................
3 f.	*i-/ta-*....................	*u-/tu-*....................
2 m.	*ta-*....................	*tu-*....................
2 f.	*ta-*....................*-ī*	*tu-*....................*-ī*
1 c.	*a-*....................	*u-*....................
Du. 3 c.	*i-*....................*-ā*	*u-*....................*-a*
Pl. 3 m.	*i-*....................*-ū*	*u-*....................*-ū*
3 f.	*i-*....................*-ā*	*u-*....................*-ā*
2 c.	*ta-*....................*-ā*	*tu-*....................*-ā*
1 c.	*ni-*....................	*nu-*....................

Note: For the 3 f. sg. the prefix *ta-* and *tu-* are employed only in OAkk and in OA (OA only with natural f. sg., not just grammatical f. sg.); in Bab. the same prefix *i-/u-* is used for both genders without distinction, e.g. *taddin* (OAkk, Ass.) "she gave", Bab. *iddin.* Under Aramaic influence the prefix of the 3 pers. f. occurs also in LB.

The conjugation is achieved partly through prefixes, which **e**
for example in the 2. pers. correspond to the indep. pron. (cf. *ta-* with *attā)*, and partly through suffixes. In the D- and Š-stems all of the prefix vowels become *u,* so that the written distinction between 1 and 3 sg. disappears (yet for OAkk, cf. § 13a). The prefix *-i-* derives from **ya-* (§ 13a). Occasionally, (esp. OB) it becomes *e* before *r: eraggam* "he makes a

claim", beside *iraggam*; *erībam* beside *irībam* "he replaced me".

f The prefixes *ta-* and *a-* become *te-* and *e-* (§ 5 a), when prefixed to *e*-containing verbs or to verbs with initial *e*-class aleph (§ 75h), e.g. *teleqqe* "you are taking" (from *leqûm*), *ēbir* "I crossed over" (from *ebērum*), *ešteme* "I have heard" (perf. from *šemûm*).

g *Note*: In the dual (OAkk, OA) only the 3 pers. forms are attested: ^{i}/*u* - ... -*ā*. Originally, the verb formed a 2. pres. dual, which had the ending -*ā*. This 2. pers. dual later displaced the 2. pers. pl. forms, so that both genders in 2. pl. are: ^{ta}/*tu*- ...-*ā*, e.g. *taplaḫā*, orig. only "you two were afraid", but then in general "you (pl.) were afraid". Only in the later periods (occasionally already in SB) as evidence of Aramaic influence do forms like *taddinū* (**ndn*) occur beside the more frequent *taddinā*.

53

c. Tenses

The Akkadian verb has four tenses: the stative (formerly called the Permansive), which is conjugated with suffixes, and the three prefixing verbal tenses: present, preterite and perfect.

Note: Originally Akkadian probably had no true "tenses" in the traditional sense. Rather it distinguished actions that were punctiliar or durative in their aspects.

54

d. Stative[66]

a The stative can be formed not only from a verb, but also from any substantive or adjective (cf. § 52a). The stative always denotes a state, even with fientic verbs (§ 51b).

b 1. Subst.: *šarrāq* "he is (was, etc.) a thief"; *aššat* "she is a married woman" (note: not **aššat-at* !); *bēl-ēku* "I am a lord"; *sinniš-ā* "they are women"; *sinniš-ātini* (OA) "you are women".

2. Adj.: *qarrād-āku* "I am heroic", *qarrād-āt*^{a}*/i*, *qarrād-ānu,* c
etc. To a limited extent formed from participles: *nāṣir* "is a rescuer", *nāṣir-āta* "you are a rescuer", *bāni* "is a creator". *Sîn-muballiṭ* (personal name) = "the moon-god is a life-giver".

3. With the transitive fientic verbs (§ 51b) the stative often d
has a passive significance: *ālu šakin* "the city is (was) situated". In general it denotes that the action expressed in the verb has in fact come to a conclusion, but has brought about a continuing resultant state. Within the sphere of durative action it is timeless, e.g. *katim* "he is (was, will be) covered". It has an active significance with the verbs[67] *ṣabātum* "to seize", *leqûm* "to take", *maḫārum* "to receive", *našûm* "to bring", and OA also *nadāʾum* "to deposit", *lapātum* "to write", e.g. *maḫir* "he is the one who has received = is the receiver", *našʾakkunūti* (OA) "he brings to you". With intransitive fientic (§ 51b) verbs, cf. *ḫaliq* "he is a fugitive", *tebâku* "I have stood up = I am upright", *mētat* (OA) "she is dead".

When the stative takes a direct object, it often has the gen- e
eral significance "have", e.g. *mārī waldat* "she has children" (lit. "she is one having borne children"); *naḫlapta labšāku* "I have on a shirt (lit. " I am one having put on a shirt"); *šuma zakrāku* "I have a name" (lit. "I am one named with a name").

e. The Present Tense 55

The present in fientic (§ 51b) verbs expresses the durative, a
i.e., not momentary action; in general, therefore, it corresponds to our pres. and future, e.g. *išappar* "he is sending" or "he will send". On the other hand, with "stative" (qualitative)

verbs the present is always ingressive (e.g., *idammiq* "is becoming good") in contrast to the stative, which designates the condition (*damiq* "is good").

b Often the present should be translated as "can...", "want(s) to ...", or "may ...", e.g. *išappar* "he may send". With *lā* "not" it expresses prohibitions, supplanting the negative imperative (§ 60e), e.g. *lā tapallaḫ* "don't be afraid". Frequently it expresses durative action in the past, e.g. *ina pāna* ... *išapparakkum* "formerly, he used to send to you".

56 *f. The Preterite Tense*

The preterite designates actual momentary, punctiliar actions. As a tense, it expresses past actions, e.g. *iṣbat* "he seized". In its original function as a punctiliar (form), it is employed for expressing wish-forms, such as in the precative (*libluṭ* "let him live"), cohortative and vetitive (cf. § 60c, d).

57 *g. The Perfect Tense*[68]

a In Akkadian the perfect is formed with infixed *-ta-*. It designates actions that have just been completed or the effects of which continue into the present (hence, frequently after adverbs *inanna* and *anumma* "now" and "henceforth", § 92b), e.g. *aṭṭardakkum* "Now I have sent to you". In the language of the later letters (MB, etc.) the perfect is used for assertions about the past based upon personal experience (cf. § 111b)[69] versus the preterite, which is used for simple statements about the past not so based. On the other hand, in negative and interrogative sentences — even in the later periods — the preterite is employed for simple past time.

b In addition the perfect can express subsequent action in the so-called c o n s e c u t i o t e m p o r u m, i.e., narrative begun in the preterite is continued in the perfect (§ 111a), e.g. *ilqē-ma ittalak* "he took and (then) went away".

Note: Since the perfect is often spelled the same way as the preterite of the *-ta-* stems (Gt, Dt, Št, Nt, etc.; § 62b), both forms can be easily confused.

h. The Ventive 58

The forms that have been enlarged by the dative suffixes a
-am and *-nim* (§ 26c sub 3) originally expressed the directional idea "to me". This suffix, which occurs chiefly with verbs of movement and of sending, often corresponds to English "here" versus "there" (movement towards the speaker).[70] For example, while forms of *alākum* without the ventive suffix have the meaning "to go (away)", those with the ventive suffix mean "to come (here)"; likewise, *inaššû* (from *našûm*) "they take away", but *inaššûnim* "they bring here".

In prose texts the ventive only occurs with verbs other than b
verbs of movement, when the verb in question is joined by the conjunctive suffix *-ma* (§ 96) with such a verb of movement, e.g. *kunkam-ma šūbilam* "seal (it) and send it here!". In poetic texts, however, it occurs also with verbs of speech: *izakkaram* "he says".

Verbal forms without vocalic suffixes take the ventive suf- c
fix *-am* (later *-a*, cf. § 18c); in plural forms with vocalic suffixes (*-ā* and *-ū*) the ventive additive is *-nim* (in later Ass. *-ne: iprusū-ne < iprusūnim*). After the ending *-ī* of the 2 f. sg. only *-m* is added (§ 26c sub 4).

Accordingly:

Sg. 3 m.	*i- ....-a(m)*	Pl.	*i- .... -ūni(m)*
3 f.	*ta- ....-a(m)*		*i- .... -āni(m)*
2 m.	*ta- ....-a(m)*		*ta- .... -āni(m)*

2 f.	*ta- .... -ī(m)*	*ta- .... -āni(m)*
1 c.	*a- ....-a(m)*	*ni- .... -a(m)*

d Ventive forms also may be constructed from imperatives (§ 59 e). In the stative the ventive is possible only in the 3 m. sg. and 3 pl.

59 ***i. Modes***

a The present, preterite, perfect and stative all distinguish indicative and subjunctive modes.

b The indicative has no special modal ending, cf. § 52b, d.

The subjunctive stands in conditional (§ 112d), relative (§ 114), and dependent, subordinate clauses (§§ 115-119).

c The subjunctive adds a *-u* to the endingless forms of the indicative, i.e., indic. *iprus,* subjunctive *ša iprusu.* After indic. forms with vocalic endings and after all forms of the ventive (§ 58c) there is no special subjunctive ending. The stative also forms the subjunctive in the same fashion. In this respect the *-at* of the 3 f. s. stative is considered an ending; hence no *-u* is added for the subjunctive form: *ša balṭat* "(she) who lives". In MB, however, the subjunctive ending *-u* is added to this form: *ša marṣatu* "(she) who is sick".

d The Assyrian dialects (but not the Babylonian ones) add to the subjunctive forms an extra particle *-ni* (also in OAkk beside *-na),* accordingly *ša išpurū-ni* (OA) "(he) who has sent" (also in the pl.). In Ass. this particle is even added to the 3 f. sg. of the stative, e.g. *damqat-ni* "(she) who is good"; and later even with both subjunctive suffixes: *balṭatū-ni,* or with the ventive ending *-am*, e.g. *ša išpuranni* "(he) who sent to me"; cf. also OAkk *adi illakanna* "until he comes".

The preterite stem without the prefixes (cf. § 63e) serves as the (2nd person) imperative. For the negated imperative, cf. § 60e. e

j. Wish- and Asseverative-Forms 60

The particle *lū* serves in the construction of the wish-form (the so-called precative), and diverging from the normal rules of construction takes a verb in the preterite. In Bab. with prefixes of the 3rd pers. — which originally were pronounced *ya*/*yu* (cf. § 13a and 52e) — *lū* becomes *lî* (in a closed syllable *li-*, § 8a), e.g. *lū* + *yablut* = *libluṭ* "may he live!"; likewise in D- and Š-stems, e.g. *lū* + *yuḫalliq* = *lîḫalliq* "may he destroy (it)!", *lū* + *yušapris* = *lîšapris*. Similarly, I *w* in the G-stem: *lū* + *ūrid* = *lîrid* "may he descend!" (root **wrd*). On the other hand, in the 1st sg. *lū* + *a*/*u* always = *lû*: *lûprus*, *lûḫalliq*, *lûšapris*. Yet in Ass. in the 1 sg. of the G-stem *lū* + *a* becomes *lâ-*: *laprus*, while in the D- and Š-stems, and also in the G-stem of I *w* verbs, the 1st sg. and 3rd sg. alike are written: *lûḫalliq*, *lûšapris*, *lûrid*. Before the prefix of the 3 f. sg. in OAkk and Ass., which begins with a consonant (cf. § 52d note), as well as before the stative (as expression of condition/state) there is no contraction, e.g. *lū taprus* "may she divide", *lū balṭāta* "may you live". a

On the other hand, the asseverative particle *lū* — outside of the royal inscriptions — does not fuse with the vowel of the prefix: *lū uḫalliq* "Verily, I destroyed" (and "I ought to have destroyed"). b

In the 1st pl. the precative is attested only in its Ass. form: *lū nišme* "we want to hear", *lū nīpuš* "we want to do." Bab. forms instead a cohortative with *i*: *i nizkur* "let us announce!"; c *i nidbub* "we wish to speak". In NB and NA the 1st pl. pret. without additional particles serves as a cohortative: NB *nidbub* "we wish to speak", NA *nillik nēmur* "let us go there and see".

d The negated wish (vetitive) is formed in Bab. through prefixing *ai* (before initial vowel) or *ē* (before consonant) to the preterite, e.g. *ai īrubū* "let them not enter"; *ai abāš* "let me not be disgraced"; *ē tašḫutī* "let not yourself (f.) be timid". In Ass., however, the prefix is *e* in all circumstances: OA *ē iqbi* "he ought not to say". Double negation expresses a positive wish[71]: *ē lā tušēbilam* "don't neglect to send"; *ē lā tašqul* "you shall surely pay".

e The prohibitive replaces the negated imperative: *lā tapallaḫ* "don't be afraid!" In NA there is no formal distinction between prohibitive and vetitive; these are both expressed by means of *lū, lā,* i.e., simple *lā* with the present tense, e.g. *lū lā amūat* "let me not die"; *lā itūar* "let him not turn back".

61 *k. Verbal Nouns*

a The infinitive (cf. § 109) is in Akkadian a substantive that can be declined. In the G-stem it is formed according to the noun pattern *parās* (cf. § 36d sub 8); in the derived stems it has *u* in the last stem syllable and thus resembles the verbal adjective (see § 61c).

Note: In the royal inscriptions of the Sargonids (SB) — but very rare in NA — a G-stem infinitive in the form *parīs* is attested,[72] e.g. *sakīp nakrēya* "the overpowering of my enemies" (the alternation of *a*/*i* points to the sound *ä* in Ass. cf. § 4a). In NA the form *parassu* (vowel length replaced by consonantal doubling, cf. § 14c) is also attested.

The active participle of the G-stem has the nominal form *pāris* (cf. § 36d sub 14). In the derived stems it is formed from the preterite, the pret. preformatives being replaced by *mu-*. The vowel of the last stem syllable is *i,* which in the Gt and N stems is elided, cf. § 67d, 66b. b

In contrast to the participle, the verbal adjective is passive. It principally serves to form the stative (§ 54). But it is also found construed adjectivally, e.g. *wardum ḫalqum* "an escaped slave". In the derived stems it resembles the infinitive in form (§ 61a). c

2. The Stem Modifications (§§ 62-72)

a. Survey of the Verbal Stems 62

The Semitic languages form a number of additional stems from the root of the predominantly triconsonantal verb, partly through doubling of the middle radical, partly through preformatives (formative elements). In Akkadian there are four principal stems. (cf. Parad. XV): a

1. the basic stem (German: *Grundstamm*) (abbrev.: G), which contains the unenlarged root;

2. the doubled stem (D), in which the middle radical is doubled;

3. the Š-stem (Š) or causative stem, before whose root the prefix *š(a)-* is appended;

4. the N-stem (N) or passive stem, before whose root the prefix *n(a)-* is appended.

In addition there exists (quite rare) an R-stem (R); with reduplication of the middle radical.

All these stems can be enlarged by infixed syllables inserted after the first radical: b

-ta-: Designation of the enlarged stems as Gt, Dt, Št (an Nt-stem is not conclusively demonstrated[73]), and Rt;

-tan-: Designation of the enlarged stem as Gtn, Dtn, Štn, Ntn and Rtn.

The ŠD-stem is restricted to the "hymnic-epic" dialect.

Note: the stems G, D, Š, N are designated in the CAD by the Roman numerals I-IV. The stems formed by the infixes *-ta-* and *-tan-* are indicated by I_2, I_3, II_2, II_3, etc.

63 ### *b. The Basic Stem (***Grundstamm***) (G)*

a The G-stem contains the unenlarged root. The final syllable has the root vowel that is characteristic for the individual semantic classes (cf. § 51b).[74] The "stative" (not stative tense!) verbs usually have *i* as a root vowel (e.g., *idammiq* "becomes good"), less frequently *a* (e.g., *ipšaḫ* "he was calm") and quite rarely *u* (e.g., *ibluṭ* "he lived", Ass. on the contrary with the root vowel *a*: *iballaṭ, iblaṭ).*

b The fientic (§ 51b) verbs from triconsonantal roots form four root classes. Many verbs have *a* in the present and perfect, *u* in the preterite: *iparras, iptaras, iprus* "to divide" (so-called "ablaut class"). The second class (*a* -class) has *a* as root vowel in all three tenses (pres., perf., pret.): *iṣabbat*, **iṣtabat, iṣbat* "to seize". The third class (*i* -class) with *i* as root vowel expresses a momentary resultative action: *ipaqqid, iptaqid, ipqid* "to hand over, commit". The fourth class (*u* -class) with *u* as root vowel designates non-momentary occurrences and actions: *irappud, irtapud, irpud* "to run".

Note: Some verbs take different root vowels according to the dialect: e.g. *erēšum* "to seed (a furrow)"; OAkk and Ass. *a/u* (ablaut class) (*erraš, ēruš)*, Bab. *i/i* (*irriš, īriš)*.

The present distinguishes itself from the preterite in that it has a stressed *a* (sometimes *e*, § 5a) after the first radical, while in the preterite the first radical is vowelless. The middle radical is doubled in the present, e.g. *iparras* "he is dividing", *iprus* "he divided"; *iṣabbat* "he is seizing", *iṣbat* "he seized"; *ipaqqid* "he is handing over", *ipqid* "he handed over" . **c**

The root vowel in the perf. of the G-stem corresponds to that of the pres., e.g. *iptaras, iptaqid, irtapud* etc. In Ass. the unstressed *-ta-* infix undergoes vowel harmony (§ 5b), yielding *iptiqid, irtupud.* When the endings are added, the root vowel is elided (§ 7a): **iptárasū* becomes *iptarsū.* **d**

The imperative resembles the root of the verb without the affixes, but the originally vowelless first syllable receives a short vowel homophonous with that of the second syllable; thus preterite *ta-prus,* imperative *purus*; *ta-pqid: piqid*; *ta-ṣbat*: *ṣabat* (cf. Parad. XIV). Exceptions can be found with preterites having *a* root vowels: *ta-lmad*: *limad* "learn!" Similarly *rikab* "ride!", *pilaḫ* "fear!", *tikal* (beside *takal*) "trust!" When endings are added, the unstressed vowel of the second syllable (even though it was the original vowel!) is elided: **purus-ī* (2.f.s.) becomes *pursī, *limad-ā* (2 pl.) becomes *limdā.* **e**

The stative has *a* in the first syllable, in the second *i* (OA *a),* cf., *šakin* "is placed", *wašib* "he sits" (OA *wašab*), *ḫaliq* "is lost" (OA *ḫalaq)*; with the "stative" verbs the second vowel is *a* or *u,* e.g. *rapaš* "is wide:, *maruṣ* "is ill". When endings are added, the short, unstressed vowel of the second syllable is elided (§ 7a): **šákinū* "they have been placed" becomes *šaknū.* **f**

g For the formation of verbal nouns (infinitive, participle and verbal adj.) in the G-stem, cf. § 61.

64 *c. The Doubled Stem (D)*

a In the D-stem the second radical is always doubled, even if the doubling is sometimes not represented in the writing (§ 3d). Unlike the G-stem, all preformatives contain the vowel *u*. The tenses are distinguished in that the present has *a*, but the preterite, perfect, imperative and participle have *i* after the doubled middle radical. The vowel *a* stands in the first syllable of the root in all tenses: *uballaṭ* "he makes alive", *uballiṭ* and *ubtalliṭ* "he has made alive". In the pret., perf. and participle from MB on, one occasionally finds *e* in the first syllable (§ 5a); thus beside *urappiš* also *ureppiš* "he made wide".

b The imperative in Ass. is regularly formed from the preterite stem (§ 59e): *tu-balliṭ* imperative *balliṭ*. In Bab., however, the first syllable contains *u,* thus *bulliṭ*.

c Infinitive and stative have *u* in both first and second syllables: *bulluṭ-um* (inf.) and *bulluṭ* (stat.). In Assyrian, however, the first syllable contains *a*: *balluṭ-um* and *balluṭ*. The first syllable of the participle (for formation, cf. § 61b) contains *a*; the second *i: mu-balliṭ-um.*

d In the "stative" verbs the D-stem denotes f a c t i t i v e action, i.e., the effecting of the condition or state denoted by the stative of the G-stem, e.g. *baliṭ* "he is alive", *bulluṭum* "to make alive"; *dān* "he is strong", *dunnunum* "to make strong".

e In the transitive fientic (§ 51b) verbs, the D-stem denotes an action that contains a plural element, perhaps executed on several objects, etc., e.g. *išber* "he broke", *ušebber* "he broke many". A number of verbs (some of them intransitive) that have a durative meaning, such as *suppûm, sullûm* "to pray", *kullum* "to hold" are only attested in the D-stem. Occasionally, the D-stem has resultative force: *ṭarādum* "to send", *ṭurrudum* "to chase away".

f The D-stem also serves to form denominative verbs (§ 51c) e.g. *ruggubum* "to roof something" from *rugbum* "roof"; *kurruṣum* "to slander" from *karṣum* "slander".

65 d. The Š-stem (Š)

a In the Š-stem the preformative *ša-* (OAkk *śa-*, cf. § 20a) is prefixed to the root. The pron. verbal prefixes contain the vowel *u*.

b The verbal stem appears in its short form after the preformative *ša-*, i.e., without a vowel between the first two radicals: *ušadgil* "he caused to see / look".

c As in the D-stem the present has *a* while the preterite, perfect, imperative and participle have *i* after the second radical. The *a* of the preformative *ša-* (beginning in MB) occasionally becomes *e* (§ 5a) in the preterite: *ušakniš* or *ušekniš* (cf. also § 64a) "he subjected". The infix *-ta-* of the perfect immediately follows the consonants of the preformative; thus *uštapris*. In MB and MA *-št-* then becomes *-lt-* (§ 20b), in NA it becomes *-ss-*, thus *ultapris* (MB/MA) and *ussapris* (NA).

d In Ass. the imperative is formed from the preterite (§ 59e), thus *šakniš* corresponds to *tu-šakniš*; but in Bab. the first syllable contains *u*, i.e., *šukniš*.

e The infinitive and stative have — as in the D-stem — a *u* vowel in the first and second syllables: *šuknuš-um šuknuš*; but in Ass. the forms are *šaknuš-um, šaknuš*. The participle is vocalized: *mu-šakniš-um* (cf. § 61b).

f The Š-stem is usually causative in force, e.g. *ušamqit* "he causes to fall". With the "stative" verbs (as in the D-stem) it has a factitive force, e.g. *šūrukum- = urrukum* "to lengthen", *šamruṣāku* (OA) "I have been made ill". Rarely its meaning may even be inchoative: *ušalbir* "he causes to become old" or "he became old" (i.e., "he made an old-becoming").

66 *e. The N-stem*

a The *n* of the stem preformative, when it is brought into immediate juxtaposition with the first consonant of the verbal root, assimilates according to the rules of § 16b to the following consonant, e.g. *ipparis* from **inparis* (pret.) "he was separated", *ittapras* (perf.) from **intapras*. The pres. and perf. of verbs of the ablaut or *a* class (§ 63b) have *a*, while the preterite has *i* in the last (theme vowel) syllable. Verbs of the *i* -class have (in all prefixed forms) *i* in the final syllable; those of the *u*- class have *a* in the pres. and perf. and *i* in the preterite (e.g., *issaḫar* (pres.) "he turns", perf. *ittasḫar*, pret. *issaḫir*, all from *saḫāru* "to turn"), less frequently they have *u* in all forms, e.g. pret. *innepuš* "he has been made", from *epēšum*. The vowel between the first and second radicals is always *a*.

Note: In Ass. the above mentioned *a* is subject to vowel harmony, e.g. *ippiris* (Bab. *ipparis)*; occasionally — by analogical development (cf. § 5c) — also in forms in which the *i* or *u* which bring about the harmony have been elided, e.g. *issiḫrū* (pret., 3 pl. from **issaḫirū)*.

b In the imperative, infinitive and stative, the preformative *na-* appears before the verbal stem: imp. *naplis* "look!", inf. *naprusum* and stat. *naprus* from **naparus*(*-um*). The participle is vocalized *mupparsum* (from **mu-n-páris-um* with elision of the *i*).

With the fientic (§ 51b) verbs N has passive force, e.g. *ipparis* "he was separated", OA *nalputāku* (**lpt)* "I have been enrolled". Several verbs have a reflexive meaning, e.g. *ittalbaš* (perf.) "he clothed himself". The N-stem of the "stative" verbs is ingressive, e.g. *annadir* (**ndr)* "I became enraged" from the adj. *nadrum* "enraged", *ibbašši* "it originates" from *bašûm* "to be". In the case of several verbs, such as *ippalis* "he looked", the N-stem takes the place of the G. c

f. The G-stem with -ta- *Infix (Gt)* 67

The Gt-stem is formed through the insertion of the infix *-ta-* after the first radical; the root vowel ("theme-vowel") corresponds to the root vowel of the G present: pres. *iptarras* after G *iparras*, pret. *iptaras,* perfect *iptatras*; pres. *imtaqqut* "he falls" after G pres. *imaqqut,* pret. *imtaqut* (Ass. *imtuqut*, cf. § 63d), perf. *imtatqut*, etc. One will observe that the preterite forms of the Gt coincide with the perf. of the G-stem. And since the writing often fails to show doubling, the pres. and pret. often are not outwardly distinguished. a

The Gt imperative has the root vowel of the Gt between the 2nd and 3rd radicals: *pitlaḫ* "fear!", *mitlik* "take counsel!" b

The inf. is vocalized *pitrusum, mitlukum,* the stative *pitrus,* in OA before vocalic endings often *pitarsum,*[75] *e.g. litabšum* "to clothe oneself", *šitapkum* "to heap up"; stative pl. *pitarsū,* e.g. *ritagmū* "they are making charges against each other." In the participle the syncopated form *muptarsum* derives from **muptarisum.* c

d The Gt stem of a number of verbs carries a reciprocal meaning: *qerēbum* "to draw near", *qitrubum* "to draw near to one another"; *maḫāṣum* "to hit", *mitḫuṣum* "to hit each other" = "to do battle"; *mitlukum* "to take counsel together." With other verbs the *t*-form serves to denote movement away from some point of reference, e.g. *alākum* "to go" *atlukum* "to go away"; with still others it denotes doing something permanently, e.g. *šitkunum* "to set something up permanently."

68 *g. The D-stem with* -ta- *Infix (Dt)*

a The Dt distinguishes itself from the D by the *-ta-* inserted after the first radical: pres. *uptarras,* pret. *uptarris*, perf. *uptatarris,* imp. *putarris,* inf. *putarrusum*, part. *muptarrisum.* Because of the passive meaning of the Dt, it does not form a stative or verbal adjective.

b The Dt serves principally as a passive for the D-stem, e.g. *uptaṭṭir* "he was loosed"; rarely it has a reflexive force, e.g. *uštabba* (OA, from *šb*ʾ) "he will satisfy himself."

c Occasionally (only in NA) Dtt forms are found, such as *uktataṣṣar* "he is outfitted". In NA the Dtt is consistently the passive for the D-stem.

69 *h. The Š-stem with the* -ta- *Infix (St)*

a The infix *-ta-* is inserted — as in the perf. of the Š-stem (§ 65c) — immediately after the consonant of the stem preformative, whereby even here in the later periods of the language *št* often becomes *lt,* which in turn becomes *ss* in NA (§ 20b). The pattern of vowels corresponds to that of the simple Š-stem: pres. *uštapras,* pret. *uštapris,* perf. *uštatapris*, inf. *šutaprusum*, etc. In the pres. the passive Št is formed on the pattern *uštapras*, whereas the "lexical" Št follows the pattern *uštaparras* (with doubled second radical).

The first Št type (Št[1]) functions as a passive of the causative Š-stem, e.g. *ušalpit* (**lpt)* "he destroyed", *uštalpit* "he was destroyed". The "lexical" Št (Št[2]) can be formed from intransitive verbs, e.g. *šutānuḫum* "to exert oneself" from *anāḫum* "to be tired"; with still other verbs its function is the causative of the reciprocal Gt-stem, e.g. *uštatamḫir* (perf.) "he made them to correspond to each other", i.e., "he squared them (mathematically)". Several verbs have an active meaning in the Št,[76] e.g. *šutēšurum* (lex. Št. from **yšr)* "to hold in order", *šutassuqum* (**nsq)* "to hold in an exceptional condition." b

i. Iterative stems with -tan- *Infix* 70

Iterative stems are formed by the insertion of *-tan-* after the first radical (§ 62b), principally Gtn and Ntn, rarely also Dtn and Štn; in the case of Ntn and Štn the infix follows the consonant of the stem preformative (*š* or *n*) immediately without an intervening vowel. a

The infix *-tan-* is preserved unchanged only in the pres. of all stems, where it stands before a vowel: *ip-tan-arras, up-tan-arras,* etc.; in the pret. **ip-tan-ras* becomes (according to § 16b) *iptarras*, pl. *iptarrasū*. According to its form it resembles the pres. of the Gt stem (**iptarras,* cf. § 67a). The perf., imp., inf., part. and stative are similarly formed. Thus: *iptatarras, pitarras, pitarrusum, muptarrisum* and *pitarrus*. In all of these forms the *n* of the *-tan-* has assimilated, **iptatanras, *pitanras*, etc. b

c The corresponding forms of the derived stems are formed on analogy to the Gtn, whereby the *n* is dropped before a doubled consonant or a cluster of two consonants, thus *uptarris* (pret. Dtn) from **up-tan-(a)rris,* etc., so that these forms coincide with the corresponding ones from the Dt and Št-stems, e.g. *uštapris* can be the pret. of Štn (from **uš-tan-pris)*, but also the pret. of Št or perf. of Š-stem.

d In the Ntn stem forms like the pres. *ittanaplas* "he looks" (from **intanaplas*) arise.

e The theme vowel in the Gtn stem corresponds to that of the Gt: thus pres. *imtanaqqut* (corresponding to Gt *imtaqqut)*, pret. *iptarras* (corresponding to Gt *iptaras).* In the Dtn, Štn and Ntn the theme vowel is identical to that of the corresponding forms of the D, Š and N.

f The meaning of the *-tan-* stems is usually iterative (or habitual), which we can express with "repeatedly" or "often", e.g. *aštanapparakkum* "I am writing repeatedly to you". Forms like *limtaḫḫarū* "may they always receive" have a distributive sense.

71 ***j. The Reduplicated Stem (R)*** [77]

a The very rare R-stem is formed by reduplication of the middle radical, e.g. *lidanannin* "may he become very thick(?)" (pret. of *danānum* "to be strong"). The following infixed forms are attested: the Rt-stem (with infixed *-ta-*): *tuddanannanā* (pres.) "you will measure each other's strength"[78] and the Rtn *muktaššaššu* (part.) "the overpowering one" from *kašāšum* "to be strong". The prefix of the R and Rt is *u-* (as in the D-stem) whereas it is *i-* in Rtn, e.g. *iktanaššaššu* "he gains power again and again (over him)."

The R-stem is very close to the D-stem in both formation and meaning. Like the D-stem (§ 64e), it expresses intensification, but in an even greater way. It is only attested in a few strong and weak verbs (e.g., *utlellûm* "to go up" from *elûm,* cf. § 84b, 85d). b

k. The ŠD Stem 72

The ŠD stem is restricted to the OB and SB hymnic and epic texts (cf. § 2a). The causative preformative *š* is attached directly to the D stem. The prefix is *u*-. The ŠD occurs only in the pres., pret. and part., e.g. *ušpazzer* "he saves", *mušpazzer* "the savior". The ŠD usually reflects the meanings of the D-stem, more rarely the Š stem. a

QUADRILITERAL VERBS 73

Some roots have four radicals. They form two principal groups: the first has *š* as the first radical (so-called "š-group" and is only used in a kind of D-stem; the second group, whose second radical is always *l* or *r,* forms both an N- and Š-stem (see Parad. XVI-XVII). a

A. The Š-Stem Group. b

As the final radical, these verbs have either *r*, *l*, *m*, or *n*. An example of a strong verb from this class is *šuqallulum* "to hand", which may actually be an expanded form of the strong triconsonantal verb *šql,* by repetition of the third radical. "Stative" verbs are: *šuḫarrurum* "to be stiff" and *šuqammumum* "to be absolutely silent". The weak roots of this type have an aleph as third radical, e.g. *šukênum* "to prostrate oneself", *šupêlum* "to exchange".

The quadriliteral verbs of the Š-group are inflected like the D-stem, e.g. pres. *ušḫarrar*, pret. *ušḫarrer*; weak roots: *ušpēl* "he exchanged"; OAkk and OA with a strong ʾ, thus *ušpaʾʾil, uškaʾʾin* "he bowed down". Although they usually have a *u* prefix vowel (e.g., *ušqallal)*, the OB and OA form *išqallal* shows that the *u* is secondary.

c B. N-Stem Group.

Of this group of quadriliteral verbs only the N- and the Š-stems and the corresponding *-tan-* infixed stems are employed. The *n* has an ingressive force. With strong verbs, e.g. *nabalkutum* "to cross over", the N stem is vocalized: pres. *ibbalakkat,* pret. *ibbalkit*, perf. *ittabalkat* (later also *i* instead of *a: ibbalakkit, ittabalkit).* The iterative stem (Ntn) is vocalized in pres. *ittanablakkat,* also with *i ittanapraššid,* from *naparšudum* "to flee"; inf. *itabalkutum* beside *itablakkutum* instead of **nitab(a)lakutum.* Š inflects like the Št of the triconsonantal, except that the first radical of the quadriliteral root stands in the position where the *t* of the Št would have stood; pret. *ušbalkit* "he allows/causes to cross", inf. *šubalkutum* (cf. *šutaprusum).* In the pres., *ušbalakkat*, SB also *ušabalakkat.* Rarely also a passive Št-stem: inf. *šutabalkutum.*

3. Peculiarities among Strong Verbs (§§ 74-76).

74 *a. Peculiarities of the Strong Verbal Roots*

a Certain categories of verbs exhibit forms that deviate because of phonetic factors. These modifications largely affect only the consonants, but partially also the vowels.

b **1' Changes in Vowels.**

In Bab. for example, *a* before or after *r* can shift to *e* (cf. § 6c), whereby the *a* vowel in the neighboring syllable can often be affected, e.g. *qerēbum* "to approach" instead of Ass. *qarābum*; *šebērum* "to smash" for *šabārum.* Before *r* and *ḫ, i* often becomes *e* (cf. § 6b), e.g. *uma*ʾʾ*er* (§ 84f) "I commissioned".

2' Changes in Consonants. c

Changes in consonants can be conditioned by any of the radicals: the first, the middle or the last.

Verbs Containing Sibilants. d

a) Verbs with Initial *š*. In MB, MA and later, *š* immediately before a dental can become *l* (§ 20b): *ilṭur* from *išṭur* "he wrote"; *iltakan* from *ištakan* "he placed"; also with quadriliteral verbs of the *š*-group, cf. MA *ultaka*ʾʾ*in* (perf.) "I have prostrated myself" (from *šukênum,* § 73b). The same sound shift *š* > *l* occurs before another sibilant, e.g. *ilsi* from *išsi* "he called" (OB/OA with assimilation, *issi)* from the root **šsī*. *št* > *lt* > *ss* in NA (on this § 15c): *issakan* from *ištakan.* α

b) Verbs with Initial *s, ṣ, z*. The *t* of the infixes *–ta–* and *–tan–* assimilates regularly to the preceding sibilant (§ 15d, sec. c), e.g. *iṣṣabat* "he seized" from **iṣtabat* (often difficult to distinguish from N-stem forms); OA *assuḫur* (from **astaḫur,* § 5b) "I was delayed". In *t*- forms without prefixes metathesis takes place, e.g. *tiṣbutum* from **ṣitbutum* "to seize one another"; *tizkaram* from **zitkaram* "speak (well) of me always"; OA *tišammeā* beside *šitammeā* (Gtn imperative) from *šamā*ʾ*um* "to hear". β

c) Verbs with Medial *s* (or other sibilant) exhibit assimilation of the infixed *t* in prefixless Gt forms to the following sibilant: *ḫissas* "observe!" from **ḫitsas*; *kiṣṣur* "is joined" from **kitṣur.* γ

Verbs With Labials. e

a) Verbs with Initial *m* are mostly regular, *imtanaqqut* (Gtn) "he falls again and again". In later Bab. *mt* often be- α comes *md* or *nd* (§ 18e): *amdaḫiṣ* “I fought” (irregular Gt pret.); *nindaggar* “we will reach an agreement” from *nimdaggar* (**mgr*); *mundaḫṣī/ē* “warriors” (§ 38h; from **mḫṣ*). Neo-Ass. *mt* > *tt* (§ 18e) *attaḫiṣ* “I fought”.

β b) Verbs with Medial *b, d, g* and *z* (voiced stops and sibilants) in Bab. resolve the doubling in the middle consonant into nasal plus middle cons. (*mb, nd,* etc.; for evidence of *n̊* with voiced stops in Akkad. cf. § 16c), e.g. *iman̊dad* “he measures” from *imaddad*; *inan̊zar* “he curses” from *inazzar*.

γ c) Verbs with Final *b* (in OB also tertiae *p*) show assimilation of the final *b* to the enclitic particle *-ma* (§ 17a): *ērum-ma* “I entered” from *ērub-ma*.

f Verbs containing Dentals or Liquids.

α a) Verbs with Initial *d* or *ṭ* change the *t* of the infixes *-ta-* and *-tan-* to *d* or *ṭ* (§ 15d), e.g. *aṭṭardakkum* “I sent to you”; *uddannin* (Dt) “was strengthened”.

β b) Verbs with Initial *r* in later Bab. sometimes change the *r* to *š* under certain circumstances: *ištakas* for *irtakas* “he bound”.

γ c) For the resolution of doubled *d* in verbs with medial *d*, cf. above § 74eβ.

g Verbs containing Palatals (Velars).

a) Verbs with initial *g* change infixed *t*’s to *d*’s (§ 15d), e.g. *igdamar* “he completed”.

b) In Ass. *t* immediately following *q* becomes *ṭ* (§ 15d), e.g. *aqṭirib* “I drew near”; and *iqṭibi* “he said”, Bab. *iqtabi*.

75 ***b. Verbs with initial aleph (I ʾ)***

a Verbs with initial aleph (I ʾ) are usually classified as strong verbs with phonetic peculiarities. They are divided into two groups, depending on the original character of the laryngeal: to the first group belong verbs with ʾ$_1$ and less often ʾ$_2$ (so-called *a*- class); to the second belong the verbs with ʾ$_3$, ʾ$_4$ and ʾ$_5$ and a few verbs with ʾ$_2$ (the so-called *e*-class).

1' The First Group (see Paradigms XVIII and XX): b

ʾ at the end of a syllable elides and the syllable vowel lengthens to compensate for its loss; thus in Bab. *i*ʾ in the pret. of the G stem becomes *ī* in *īkul* "he ate"; Ass., however, *ē* (§ 14d): *ēkul* from **iʾkul*; *nībut* "we destroyed" from **niʾbut*; *ābut* "I destroyed" from **aʾbut*; perf. *ātabat* from **aʾtabat*; *ītaḫaz* (Bab.) "he has seized", Ass. *ētaḫaz*; Dt *ūtaḫḫiz* "he was seized" from **uʾtaḫḫiz*; Š *ušābit* "he had (it) destroyed" from **ušaʾbit*; stat. *šūkul* "is foddered" from **šuʾkul*. Between vowels (in pres. G-stem and in the D-stem) ʾ together with the following vowel usually drops: *ikkal* "he eats" (OB written *i-ik-ka-al,* cf. § 14a) from **iʾakkal,* Ass. *ekkal*; in D pres. *uḫḫaz* "he plated/overlaid" (OB written *ú-uḫ-ḫa-az),* pret. *uḫḫiz* (OB written *ú-uḫ-ḫi-iz*) from *aḫāzum* "to seize, marry".

In the verb *alākum* "to go" (with *a*/*i* theme vowel pattern like the I *w* roots) the syllable-closing ʾ assimilates to the following consonant (§ 14c): *illik* "he went" from **iʾlik* (pres. *illak*, cf. section b); Gt *ittalak* "he went forth" from **iʾtalak*, Gtn pres. *ittanallak.* On the other hand, the Š stem follows the regular pattern for I ʾ verbs: pret. *ušālik,* inf. *šūlukum,* etc. c

For some verbs (like *abātum* "to destroy") Bab. forms can be found with a strong ʾ: pres. *iʾabbat,* pret. *iʾbut* beside regular *ibbat, ību*t; in the D pres. *uʾabbat,* pret. *uʾabbit*, part. *muʾabbitum* beside *ubbat, ubbit, mubbitum*. Cf. also d

OAkk/OA *uʾaḫḫ^a/er* (**ʾḫr* "to remain behind") "he is (was) late", vs. regular Bab. *uḫḫ^a/er* (for *i* > *e* before *r* cf. § 6b).

e The G imp. is formed from the preterite stem with an initial helping vowel *a*: *akul* "eat!", *alik* "go!" Similarly, *i* becomes *a* after ʾ in the Gt imp. and inf., e.g. *atkaš* "go forth!" from *akāšum*, with ventive *atalkam*; inf. *atlukum* "to go away" from *alākum*; NA imp. *litanka*.[79]

f In the pres. of Š and Št, syllable-ending ʾ assimilates to the following consonant, whereby the middle radical is doubled (analogous to the G stem): *ušaḫḫaz* and *uštaḫḫaz*.

g In the N-stem ʾ assimilates to the *n*: *innamer* "he was seen" (also reciprocal: "he met with [another person]") from **inʾamer*. Accordingly the inf. is *nanmurum*, beside less frequent *nāmurum* from **naʾmurum*. With the verb *abātum* (with strong ʾ) forms occur in which the *n* of the N stem assimilates to the ʾ, producing ʾʾ: pres. *iʾʾabbat* "will be destroyed", pret. *iʾʾabit*; likewise with *adārum* "to fear": pres. *iʾʾaddar*, pret. *iʾʾadir* (Ass. *iʾʾidir*).

Note: Beside *iʾʾabbat* and *iʾʾabit* there is also an N stem (probably from *ʾbt* II, see AHw sub *nābutu*): *innabbit, innabit* with the meaning "to flee".

h **2' The Second Group (see Paradigms XIX and XXI):**

If the aleph is $ʾ_3$, $ʾ_4$ or $ʾ_5$, any *a* before or after it will become *e* (§ 6a); furthermore, in Bab. other neighboring *a*ʾs under the influence of the newly formed *e* also become *e* (§ 5a): *ēbir* "I crossed" from **aʾbir*, *ētebir* from **aʾtabir*, *ušēbir* from **ušaʾbir*, etc. But in Ass. (and OAkk) the *a* in the neighboring syllable is unaffected: *epāšum* "to do", Bab. *epēšum*; *erāšum* (OAkk, OA also *arāšum*) "to plant", Bab. *erēšum*; *ētarab* "I (have) entered", Bab. *ēterub*, etc. The syllable *i*ʾ in both the first (*a*-class) and the second (*e*-class) groups becomes *ī* in Bab. and *ē* in Ass. (§ 14d), e.g. Bab. *īrub* "he entered", Ass. *ērub*.

The verb *epēšum* "to do" had in OB the G pres. *ippeš* from **ippaš*, but later *ippuš*, Ass. *eppaš*; pret. Bab. *īpuš*, Ass. *ēpuš*. Likewise in the pres. of N-stem: Bab. *inneppeš* "it will be done", Ass. *inneppaš*. **i**

Just as with verbs of the Group I (*a*-class), so also in verbs of Group II (*e*-class) the Š pret. and pres. are distinguished in that the middle radical of the pres. is doubled; pres. *ušezzeb* (§ 5a) "he has (a document) drawn up, he saves/rescues" (from *ʾ*zb*), beside pret. *ušēzib*; *ušerreb* (Ass. *ušerrab*) beside pret. *ušērib*; *ušeppeš* (Ass. *ušeppaš*) beside pret. *ušēpiš*. **j**

3. *Verbs with medial aleph* (II ʾ) **76**

Verbs with medial aleph (II ʾ), like I ʾ verbs, distinguish two classes or groups (cf. Parad. XXII): to Group I belong verbs with ʾ$_{1-2}$; to Group II belong those that color *a* to *e*. A few verbs fluctuate between the two classes (e.g., *nârum*/*nêrum* "to kill"; root **nʾr*, cf. § 84d). **a**

A. To Group I (without *a* > *e* shift) belong verbs that retain a strong pronunciation of the ʾ as well as those that do not. Examples of strong: *iraʾʾub* "he becomes angry", *idaʾʾum* "it becomes dark", pret. *idʾim* (written in OB *id-ḫi-im*). **b**

Examples of weak inflection: *râmum* "to love", pres. *irâm* (pl. *irammū*), perf. *irtām*; *šâlum* "to ask", pret. *išāl* (Bab.), later often *išʾal* (Ass.); *šâmum* "to buy", pret. *išām*, OA strong *išʾam* (cf. *ša išʾumu* "who bought"). In the G-stem they follow the analogy of verbs with medial *a* (so-called "hollow roots", § 82), e.g. *ibār* "he caught" (for **ibʾar*), like *ibāš* **c**

(§ 82b) “he was ashamed”; *ibarrū* “they caught” (for *iba*ʾʾ*arū)*. In MB the ʾ is often restored.

d B. Group II (with *a* > *e* shift): These verbs too inflect like the hollow roots (*mediae ē*; § 82c); but instead of *a* as in *ibār, e* appears (according to § 6a): pres. *ibêl* “he rules” (pl. *ibellū*), pret. *ibēl,* pl. *ibēlū* for **ib*ʾ*elu,* in the oldest periods and in Ass. still inflected strongly: *ibe*ʾʾ*al* (OAkk), *ib*ʾ*el* (Ass.), inf. *be*ʾ*ālum,* Bab. *bêlum.*

e In the D-stem one finds contracted forms in the Bab. pres., e.g. *ušâl* (*a*-class) “he inquired”, *urêq* (*e*-class) “he made remote”, NA on the other hand with a strong ʾ, e.g. *uba*ʾʾ*aš* “he makes something bad”; in pret. and perf. also Bab. uncontracted forms: *uša*ʾʾ*il, ušta*ʾʾ*il.*

f After the model of the hollow roots the Š stem is formed with prefixed *š*- instead of *ša-,* e.g. *ušnēš* (*e*-class) “he let live” (from *nêšum* “to live”). Occasionally formed as strong verbs: pres. *ušam*ʾ*ad,* pret. *ušam*ʾ*id,* inf. *šum*ʾ*udu* beside *šumūdum.*

g The N-stem is usually formed weak like the hollow roots, i.e., pres. *iššâl, ibbêl*; pret. *iššāl, ibbēl.*

Note: For the final weak verbs (III ʾ) see § 83.

4. The Weak Verb (§§ 77-86)

77

a. General Observations on the Weak Verb[80]

a Those verbs whose roots originally consisted of only two consonants are called weak verbs. Biconsonantal roots can have a long vowel between the two consonants (so-called hollow roots) or after the second radical (so-called final weak verbs) If the vowel is short, the biconsonantal base is expanded either through gemination of the second radical or by making it triconsonantal by prefixing a root augment such as *w(a)-* or *n(a)-*. With the exception of the verbs with a doubled second radical, which have almost completely assimilated themselves to the triconsonantal roots, the weak verbs exhibit many deviations from the forms discussed in §§ 63-70.

The individual groups of the fientic (§ 51b) weak verbs form semantic classes. **b**

b. Verbs with n *as First Radical (I* n*)* 78

The root augment *n(a)-* of the I *n* verbs is a semantic-class-forming element and in many cases expresses direction, e.g. *nadānum* "to give", *nadûm* "to put there", *našûm* "to carry". Other verbs are onomatopoetic: *nabāḫum* "to bark, make the sound *buḫ*". In several verbs like *nadārum* "to be angry" the *n* is an original part of the root, i.e., the verb is morphologically strong. **a**

The *n* assimilates (paradigm XXIII) to the following consonant (§ 16b), e.g. *iddin* "he gave" from **indin, aqqur* "I tore down" from **anqur*; Ass. *attumuš* (perf. cf. § 5b) "I set out" from **antamuš* (root **nmš*). In the Š and the Št the *n* is sometimes restored (probably as the secondary palatal *n*, § 16c): *ušanzaq* = *ušazzaq* "he provoked". Likewise in N, e.g. *nanqur* (stative) beside *naqqur*. **b**

The imperative in Ass. is formed on a biconsonantal base. Thus *din* "give!" *diā* (root **ndī*, cf. § 84e) "put!", beside *idʾā*. In Bab. the root vowel is prefixed, as in *idin, uqur*, etc. In the imp., inf. and stat. of the Gt and Gtn stems the initial *n* is dropped, e.g. *itpuṣum* "to be smashed" instead of **nitpuṣum*; OA *ana itaṭlim* (from **nṭl)* "for mutual consideration" — that **c** is, "for cash"; *itakkis* imp. Gtn from *nakāsum* "to cut off," instead of **nitakkis*.

d In Ass. the pres. *iddan* (pl. *iddunū)* is formed from the pret. *iddin* by means of internal vowel alteration; in Babyl, the pres. is regular *inaddin* (secondarily *ina*^{m}*/ndin,* cf. § 16c), OAkk *inaddan*. The inf. and the stat. in Ass. reflect a secondary root **tdn: tadānum, tadin* (cf. § 80b). All other roots show regular formations.

e *Note*: In the verb *nadānum* in MB/LB[81] the *d* often assimilates to the following *n* (§ 15d), cf. MB *ittannaš-šum-ma* (perf. G) "he has given to him and ..." from **intadin-am-šum-ma*; LB *innā* "give!" from *idnā*; in NA G perf. *ittannū* from **intadinū*, **ittadinū*.

79

c. Verbs with Identical Second and Third Radical

a As a semantic class, fientic verbs (§ 51b) with identical second and third radical have a durative connotation, often in an iterative sense (the so-called "chain durative" [German *Kettendurativ*]), e.g. *šadādum* "to drag", *šakākum* "to line up," *dabābum* "to speak". They follow almost entirely the scheme of the triradical strong verb. Only the verbs with stative meanings form their stative on the pattern of the weak verbs, so *dān* "he is strong" (from *danānum*). Fem. *dannat* (like *parsat*), *sār* "it is fraudulent" (from *sarārum), ēd* "it is sharp" (from *edēdum*) beside *ṣalil* "he sleeps".

b Some verbs, whose doubled radical is an *l* or an *r*, form the N-stem according to the scheme **naparrurum*, as e.g. *nagarruru* "to roll over" (from *garārum* "to bend oneself"); *naḫallulu* "to crawl" (from *ḫalālu* "to rustle, whisper"), etc. They have an ingressive-durative meaning.[82]

d. Verbs with w *as First Radical (I* w*)* 80

a Fientic verbs that are expanded from biconsonantal roots with the addition of *w(a)-* (parad. XXV) sometimes denote movement towards a goal (*wabālum* "to carry" *wašābum* "to seat oneself there") and sometimes movement emerging from point of origin (*waṣûm)* (§ 84 g) "to go forth"). In the case of the "stative" verbs, which distinguish no semantic classes, the *w* probably belongs to the root, e.g. *waqārum* "to be valuable", *watārum* "to be in excess". These latter are treated (§ 81) like the I *y* roots (§ 80g).

b *Note*: The *w* that was still preserved in OB later usually becomes ʾ, more rarely *m*: *walādum* "to bear", later *alādum* or *malādu*. (Concerning **mʾr* < **nʾr*, cf. § 84f). Some verbs that were originally biconsonantal are expanded into triconsonantal strong verbs by a root augment *ta-* (§ 78d): *wabālum/tabālum, wašābum/tašābum* (on imp. cf. § 80e).

c A. In the case of the fientic verbs (§ 51b), the diphthongs *aw-* and *iw-* of the prefixes become *ū-* (§ 12c), thus *ūšib* "I sat down" from **awšib* (pret.) *ūbil* "he brought" from **yawbil*. The present has a theme vowel *a* in the last syllable and doubles the middle radical: *uššab* (therefore ablaut class *a/i* as in the I ʾ verb *alāku,* cf. § 75c). In the pret. elision (§ 7a) often occurs: *ublam* for *ūbilam* "he brought here".

d In OAkk the perf. was formed from the biconsonantal base with the prefixed *t,* thus: *itbal* (still in the Code of Hammurapi), but in most OB and later from the secondary root with root augment *t(a)-*, e.g. *ittarad* "he descended, went down". In later Assyrian the perfect was formed anew on the basis of the pret. G: *ittūšib* (cf. *ūšib)*, Bab. *ittašab* .

e In the G imp. the root appears without its root augment: *bil* "carry!", *šib* "sit down!", but also *tišab* (from *tašābum* with the augment *ta*-, cf. § 80b).

f In the rest of the prefixless forms (inf., part., stative) in MB and later the *w* of the root augment disappears (§ 80b): *wālidum* "begetter", later *ālidu*. The part. of **wbl* is formed (like the inf.) from the secondary root **bbl*: *bābilum, babālum* (§ 12b, note); yet often in Mari and always in OA, *wābilum*. In Ass. the initial *wa*- occasionally becomes *u*- (§ 12a): Bab. *wašbat* "she sits" OA *ušbat* beside *wašab*; MA and NA *ulādu* (inf.); D stem: OA *wattur* "(is) valuable" beside *uttur*.

g B. The "stative" verbs like *waqārum* (all with theme vowel *i*) inflect in the pres. and pret. like the I *y* verbs (§ 81), thus: *iqqer, īqer*; perf. *ītaqer,* wherein the *a* vowel of the infix is preserved.

h In the derived stems the fientic (§ 51b) and stative verbs behave identically. The D stem usually inflects in a strong fashion, e.g. *tuwattar* "you are making something excessive", perf. *tūtatter*. Yet weak formations also occur, e.g. *uttar* (pres.), *utter* (pret.).

i In the Š stem prefixless forms in Bab. are: *šūšubum* (inf.) "to place" from **šuwšubum*; *šūbil* (imp.) "have (something) brought!" In the forms with prefixes they are like I ʾ verbs: pres. *ušaššab* (doubling of second radical like *ušakkal,* § 75f), pret. *ušāšib* (like *ušākil*), *ušāpi* "he created" (§ 84g); often though also like I *y* verbs (§ 81c): *ušēšib* (from **ušayšib*), *ušēpi*. In Ass. the forms with *e* are the rule: *ušēbil* "he had something brought", perf. *uštēšib,* imp. *šēšib,* part. *mušēšibum,* etc.

Forms with *ū* like *ušūpiū* "they beautified", "they created" from **ušawpiū* are only attested in the older language. **j**

In the N the *n* becomes ʾ in the later lang.: *iʾʾaṣṣab* "is added", *iʾʾalid* "was born", from older *iwwalid* (from **inwalid*) still preserved in the older language. The N of *wabālum* is formed from the secondary root **bbl* (see sect. f above): *ibbabbal, ibbabil.* **k**

e. Verbs with y *as First Radical* **81**

The I *y* verbs inflect like the *e-* class of the I ʾ verbs (paradigm XXVI), e.g. *ēniq* "I sucked", but 3rd pers. Bab. and Ass. *īniq,* pres. *inniq*; similarly *ēṣip* "I doubled", *ēṣir* "I formed"; *īšer* (§ 6b) "he went up ... to", pres. *iššer*. Other forms also are formed on analogy with the I ʾ *e-* class verbs, cf. inf. *eṣēpum, ešērum,* OA *išārum,* stat. *eniq*. **a**

In the D stem they inflect as weak verbs: *uṣṣir* "he drew, inscribed", pres. *uṣṣar,* perf. *ūteṣṣir* (from *eṣērum*). **b**

In the Š the forms resemble those of the I *w* verbs, e.g. *ušēšer* "he put in order" from **ušayšir*, perf. *uštēšer* (= Št pret.), pres. *ušeššer* (cf. § 80i). **c**

In the N, the *y* assimilates to the *n* according to § 13b, e.g. *inneššer* "he will be put in order, become successful" from **inyaššer*. **d**

f. Middle Weak Verbs ("Hollow Roots") **82**

Verbs that have a long vowel in place of a middle radical are called as Middle Weak Verbs or "hollow roots". Any of the four vowels (*ā, ē, ī,* or *ū*) can appear as theme vowel (paradigms XXVIII to XXXI). **a**

a) There are only a few verbs with *ā* theme vowel, e.g. *ibāš* (cf. Heb. "he became ashamed". Some verbs with medial **b** aleph, such as *ibār* (§ 76c), also inflect on analogy with hollow roots with an *ā* theme vowel.

c b) Verbs with medial *aleph* of the *ē*- class are also counted with hollow verbs of theme vowel *ē, e.g. ibêl* "he is ruling" (§ 76d).

d c) Of the highest frequency are hollow verbs with theme *ū*. Fientic verbs (§ 51b) of this type often denote the sudden transition from one condition to the opposite or the causing of such a sudden transition, e.g. *dâkum* "to kill", *târum* "to turn around". Other verbs entail durative movement, e.g. *šâdum* "to hunt about", *sârum* "to dance", etc.

e d) Hollow verbs with theme *ī* serve to denote terminative actions (e.g., *diānum* "to pronounce a verdict", *qiāšum* "to bestow, confer") or bodily functions (e.g., *šiānum* "to urinate", *ṣiāḫum* "to laugh").

f "Stative" verbs having hollow roots with *ū* and *ī* themes form no semantic classes, e.g. *ṭiābum* "to be beautiful, good".

g G-stem: the bare root appears in the imp. *dūk* "kill!", pl. *dūkā*; *šīm* "determine!" (II *ī)*, as also in the pret. *ikūn* "he became firm", pl. *ikūnū*; *idīn* "he judged". The pres. of II-*ū* verbs is vocalized *idâk* (Bab.) or *idūak* (Ass., uncontracted), OA also *itūwar* (with *w* representing the hiatus, cf. § 12c note); *inâḫ* (§ 84d) "he goes to rest", Ass. *inūaḫ*. In the pl. with doubled final radical instead of a long theme vowel: *inuḫḫū* "they are going to rest". In Bab. the perf. is formed from the pret., e.g. *imtūt* "he died", *iddūk* < **idtūk* (cf. § 15d); in Ass. on the other hand regularly from the present: *imtūat*. With II *ī* verbs uncontracted forms of the pres. are still in evidence in OB: *iqīaš* "he gives", *iṭīab* "he is becoming good", later contracted to *iqâš* (in Mari *iqêš,* cf. § 9a), *iṭâb*. Similarly the Ass. perf. is uncontracted *iqtīaš,* Bab. *iqtīš* (formed from pret.). When a (vocalic) ending follows the final radical, the latter is doubled, as in II *ū* verbs: *išimmū,* pl. to *išâm* "he is determining". In the inf. of II *ū* Bab. shows contraction: *dâkum,* Ass. without contr. *duākum*, also with *w* as hiatus marker: *ittuwārīšu* "upon his return" = Bab. *ina târīšu*; with II *ī* verbs both OB and Ass. are uncontracted: *qiāšum,* later *qâšu.* The vowel in stat. and verbal adj. of II *ū* verbs is *ī* (Bab.) or *ē* (Ass.) (both < *ai*, see § 9c): *dīk, dēk* (Ass.) "he is slain", *mītum* or *mētum* "dead"; in II *ī* verbs the vowel is *ā* or *ī*: *ṭāb* "is good", *šīḫu* "grown tall".

In Bab. the D-stem is inflected weak, in earlier Ass. strong, **h**
e.g. pret. *urīḫ* "he left over", imp. *kīn* "make (something) lasting!" (Bab.); *uqaʾʾiš* "he conferred", *ukaʾʾil* "he held", *kaʾʾin* (Ass.). In NA, on the other hand, strong and weak formations alternate:[83] *ukayyin*, *ukīl.* Similarly, (Bab.) *tēr* "turn!", (Ass.) *taʾʾer*; stat. *kūn* (Bab.), *kaʾʾun* (Ass.), *taʾʾur* (Ass.) "is given back". In Ass. only the pres. is, as in Bab., formed weak: *ubâš* "he puts to shame", *uqâš* "he gives". Unlike the strong verb (§ 64a), in the D stem the hollow roots double the final, rather than the middle, radical, when the form has a vocalic ending. Thus, instead of **utērū* (pret.) *uterrū* ("they turned") occurs, pres. *utarrū* (in similar fashion to the G pres. 3rd pl. *idukkū* compared with the 3rd sg. *idâk*), stat. *kunnū* (pl. to *kūn)* "they were convicted"; inf. *kunnum.*

The Š-stem is formed with the preformative *š-*, as in the **i**
II ʾ verbs: pret. *ušmīt* "he killed", pl. *ušmittū,* perf. *uštamīt*, pres. *ušmāt,* in OA *ušbīat* (pres.) "he makes (someone) spend the night".

j The N stem: *iddâk* "he will be put to death", in the older language *iddūak* (OA even *iddūwak*), pl. *iddukkū*; *iqqīap* "he will be trusted".

83 **g. *Final Weak Verbs (III* ʾ/w/y*)***

a To this group belong: (1) roots that consist of two consonants and that have a long vowel, *ī* or *ū,* instead of the third radical, 2) weakly inflected *tertiae aleph* verbs, among which one can distinguish two subgroups: (a) those without "umlaut" (*e* coloring of short *a* vowels), which end in *a* ($ʾ_1$), and (b) those with "umlaut" of *a* to *e,* which end in alephs 3, 4, or 5. In all of these verbs (see paradigms XXXII - XXXVI) the originally long vowel shortens in final position according to § 8a and § 23, e.g. with *ī*: *ibni* "he built"; with *ē*: *išme* "he heard"; with *ū: imnu* "he counted", *iḫdu* "he rejoiced; with *ā*: *ikla* "he restrained", *itma* "he swore". Transfers from one group to the other is frequent in the later stages of the language, cf. *amni* beside *amnu* "I counted".

b When vocalic affixes are added to the verbs of this class, in OB (and then only with verbs III *ī*/*ē* with following *a*) one finds uncontracted forms, e.g. *iqbiam* "he said to me", *ibniā* (beside *ibnâ*) "they (f.) built"; otherwise, such forms contract: *išemmû* "they hear" (OAkk as yet uncontracted *išemmeʾū),* *ikallû* (III *a)* "they hold back", *iqbû* "they said" (archaic: *iqbiū)*; in Mari *rabêt* (§ 9a) "she is large" from *rabiat.* Ass. on the contrary mostly uncontracted; *ilqeʾū* "they took", *peteʾā* "open (pl.)!", *tibʾamma* "arise and …", *zakuʾāku* (III *ū*) "I have been purified" beside *zakuwāku* (§ 12c note), Bab. *zakâku,* inf. *tamāʾum* (OA) "to swear".

The *e*- class often changes *a* in adjacent syllables into *e* (§ 5a) e.g. *išemme* "he hears" (with older *išamme*), *teleqqe* "you take" (< **talaqqe*). Such forms as the Bab. stative *šemi* (3 m. sg.) and *šemât* (3 f. sg.) may be understood to have developed through analogy. In Assyrian even the III *ē* verbs retain the *a* in the other syllables, e.g. *laqiāku* "I am taken". c

Note: With the addition of endings (suffixes, etc.), the original length of the shortened final vowel (sect. a) is restored, e.g. *ibnī-šu, ibnī-ma, išmē-ma, itmā-ma, imnū-ma*. For the declension of the inf. with pron. suffixes see § 42g. d

In the imperative the first vowel will usually correspond to the theme vowel (just as in the strong verb), e.g. *bini,* "build!" *šeme,* "hear!", *munu,* "count!", f. *punuī* (OA) "apply yourself!", but *kila* "hold!", *taru* "fetch!". e

In the D and Š stems the final vowel corresponds to the pattern of the strong verb, e.g. *ubanna* (D pres., after *uparras)* "he makes good," *umalla* "he fills"; *ubanni, umalli* (D pret.); *ušabna* (Š pres. after *ušapras*), *ušabni* (Š pret.); *uštabarri* (Št "lexical" cf. § 69a) "he waits" (from **br*ʾ "to hunger"), etc. But in the *e* class in Bab. the D pres. shows both *upette* and *upatte* "he makes arable", and the Š pres. shows both *ušepte* and *ušapte* (Ass. *ušapta*). f

Beside the regular Š stem there are the poetic ŠD forms, such as *ušmalla/i*. g

In the N stem the theme vowel appears again, e.g. *ibbanni,* "is built", *ippette* "is opened," *iššamme* (OA) "is heard", *ikkalla* "is held back", *immannu* "is numbered". h

A few III ʾ verbs are inflected as strong verbs, e.g. **pr*ʾ*: apru*ʾ "I cut off"; D *uparri*ʾ. i

84 *h. Doubly and Triply Weak Roots*

a Doubly weak verbs are those with two weak radicals, that is, an aleph, a long vowel or an intial *n, w* or *y*. Beyond this there are also verbs in which all three radicals are weak.

b 1. Verbs with initial *aleph* (I ʾ, § 75) and a final weak consonant (III ʾ/*w*/*y* § 83):

elûm (*e-* class § 75h) "to go up", (OA *elāʾum).* G pret. *īli,* pres. *illi,* perf. *īteli* (Ass. *ēli, elli, ēte*/*ili*); D *ulli,* "he exalted", perf. *ūtalli* (NA), Š *ušēli.* Similarly *enûm* "to change", *epûm* "to bake".

c 2. Verbs with initial *aleph* (§ 75), with medial *w* and with a final weak consonant:

a) *awûm* (*a*-class § 75b) "to speak". Gt pret. OB *ītawu*[84] "he discussed/conferred", (old Ass. also *ētau*), SB *ītami,* pres. *itamm*^{u}/*a,* inf. *atmû* (old *atwûm).*

b) *ewûm,* later *emû* (*e*-class) "to become". G pret. OB *īwe,* SB *īme,* perf. *īteme*; Š *ušēme.*

In both verbs the older language retains the *w*, but the later writes it with *m.*

d 3. Verbs with initial *n* (§ 78) and medial *ū*/*ī* (§ 82d,e) or II ʾ (§ 76):

nârum (*nêrum*) "to kill". G pres. *inâ*/*êr* (cf. § 76a), pret. *inār* and *inēr.*

nâḫum (§ 82g) "to come to rest". G pres. *inâḫ,* pret. *inūḫ,* perf. *ittūḫ*; D *unāḫ, unēḫ, uttēḫ*; SB participle *muniḫḫu.*[85]

nêʾum (II ʾ, Group II, § 76d), "to turn". G pret. *inē.*[86]

e 4. Verbs with initial *n* and a final weak consonant:

nabûm "to name". G pret. *ibbi* (*imbi*, cf. § 22c), perf. *ittabbi*, imp. *ibi*; similarly *nadûm* "to put", imp. OA *idʾā* beside *diā* (§ 78c) “put!”; *našûm* “to lift, transport”, imp. OA *šiā*; *naqûm* “to offer sacrifice”.

5. Verbs with initial *w(a)-* (§ 80) and a medial weak consonant: **f**

wârum “to set out” (OA *waʾārum*). D pret. *uwaʾʾer, uwēr,* “he commanded”, MB and LB *umaʾʾer* (**mʾr,* cf. § 74b).

6. Verbs with initial *w(a)-* (§ 80) and a final weak consonant: **g**

a) *wapûm* “to be visible” Š pret. *ušāpi* (Bab.) “he brought forth, created”, *ušēpi* “he glorified”, perf. *uštāpi, uštēpi.*

b) **waqûm*[87] “to wait”, in the D stem pret. *i nuwaqqi* “let us wait” (OB strong), *uqqi* (Ass. weak).

c) *warûm* “to lead”. G pret. *ūru,* perf. *itru* (OAkk, formed on a uniconsonantal base; similar to *itbal*; cf. § 80b), imp. *ru*; Gtn pret. *ittarru*; Š imp. *šūri,* OA *šā/ēriam.*

d) *waṣûm* “go out”. G pret. *ūṣi,* pres. *uṣṣi*, perf. *ittaṣi* (Ass. *ittūṣi*, cf. § 80d) imp. *ṣī*; Š pret. *ušēṣi* “he sent out, rented, leased”, pres. *ušeṣṣi*, perf. *uštēṣi.*

e) *watûm* “to find”. G pres. *utta*; Št *šutātûm* “to meet one another”.

7. Verbs with initial *y* (§ 81) and a medial weak consonant: **h**
eʾēlum (*e-* class) “to bind”, G pret. *īʾil,* D *uʾʾil.*

8. Verbs with initial *y* and a final weak consonant **i** (defective verbs that only form one aspect of the normal forms):

a) *egûm* “to become lazy”. G pret. *īgi, īgu* (1 sg. *ēgi/u*), pres. *iggu.*

b) *idûm* (Bab. **ydʾ*, Ass. **wdʾ*) “to know” G *īde* (3 and 1 s.) “he knows / I know” (NA *ūda*: pres., *ūdi*: pret.), inf. OA *idā'um*,[88] participle *mūdûm*; D pret *u wa/eddi* (strong) "he characterized" (Ass. also weak *uddi*); *ušēdi*.

c) *išûm* "to have". G pret. (w. the meaning of the stative) *īšu*, later *īši* (3 and 1 s.). Cf. § 83a.

j 9. Verbs with medial *aleph* (§ 76) and a final weak consonant:

a) *bu''ûm* "to seek", appears only in the D stem: pret. *uba''i*, perf. *ubta''i*.

b) *le'ûm* "to be able". G pres. *ile''i*, pret. *ilē*.

c) *re'ûm* "to pasture". G pres. *ire''i*, pret. *irē*; Gtn *irtene''i*. Similarly *še'ûm* "to seek", old Ass. *še'āum*. pret. *iše* (old Ass. *iš'e*), imp. *še*; Gtn *ištene''i*.

k 10. Verbs with weak second and third radicals:

a) *bâ'um* "to go along". G pret. *ibā'* beside OB *ibâ*, perf. *ibtā'*, *imp*. *bā'*; Š pres. *ušbā'*, pret. *ušbī'*, imper *šubī'*.

b) *mâ'um* (OA) with negative, "to be unwilling". G pret., *imū'a/imūwa* (cf. § 109f).

85 *i. Irregular Verbs*

To the irregular verbs belong:

a 1. *izuzzum*, *uzuzzum* "to stand" (biconsonantal root **ziz*).

The G-stem, as well as the Gt and Gtn, is formed with a prefixed *n*: pres. *izzaz* "he stands", pl. *izzazzū*, pret. *izziz*, perf. *ittaziz*. In the imp. and inf. the initial *n* disappears: imp. *iziz*, inf. *izuzzum*, with vowel harmony *uzuzzum*, OA *izēzum*.[89] Participle *muzzazzum* (Bab.) *muzzizum* (Ass.). Gt OB *ittazzaz* "he goes over to"; Gtn pres. *ittanazzaz*. Š stem pres. Bab. *ušzaz*, pret. *ušziz*, later *ulziz* (§ 20b) beside pres. *ušazzaz*, pret. *ušazziz* (Ass.), in LB *uša/ezziz*; perf. *ušta/eziz*, later *ulteziz* (§ 20b), inf. *šuzuzzum*, *imp*. *šuziz*. Štn pres. *uštanazzaz*.

The first *z* in the root **ziz* often dissimilates in later times. This apparently accounts for the root **šiz* in Babyl; **zis* and **tiz/s* in Ass. Cf. G imp. Ass. *itiz,* Bab. *išiz* = *iziz,* Bab. inf. *ušuzzu,* NA *itussu* = *uzuzzu,* Bab. perf. *ittašiz,* Ass. *ittatiz* = *ittaziz.*

2. *i/utūlum* "to lie" (root **tīl,* **nīl*). **b**

G pres. *inâl,* pret. *inīl,* stative *nīl* (OA *nāl*) from the root **nīl,* beside pret. *ittīl,* inf. *itūlum* (frequently with assimilation of the *i*: *utūlum*), stat. *utūl* from the root **tīl.* Š pres. *ušnâl,* pret. *ušnīl* (also *ušnaʾil),* imp. *šunīl,* stat. *šunūl.*

3a) *naʾādum* (I *n* and *mediae aleph*) "to watch, be aware". **c**

G pres. *inaʾʾid,* pret. *iʾʾid,* perf. *ittaʾid,* imp. *iʾid.* D *unaʾʾad* "he makes (someone) aware", imp. *nuʾʾid,* etc.

b) *nâdum* "to praise" (hollow root, II *ā*). pret. *inād,* imp. *nād.* The D stem is inflected like the D of *naʾādum.*

4a) *utlellûm* (on this see § 71b) "to arise" (from *elûm*). G pret. *ūtelelli,* imp. *utlellî,* participle *mutlellûm.* **d**

b) *utnennu* "to pray", SB and LB pret. *utnēn,* participle *mutnennû.*

Defective Verbs **86**

a The verbs *idûm* "to know" and *išûm* "to have" are defective (see on this § 84h). So also is *laššu* (from *lā-iššu*) "is not", which on rare occasions in OA inflects (*laššuāku* "I am not").[90]

b The pronominal form *ayyānu(m)* (Bab.) "where?" (cf. § 91a) may be classed as a defective verb, since by MB it had been transformed into a kind of unconjugated stative: *yānu, yaʾnu* "is not, are not".

87 Verbs with Suffixes

a The pronominal suffixes are attached to the verbal forms and combine with them to form a single word (see paradigms XXXVII-XXXVIII). The verbal pronominal suffixes distinguish dative and accusative (see § 26b).

b The 1 sg. dative suffix is formally and objectively identical with the ventive ending *-am* (§ 58a). Cf. *tašpuram* = 1. "You sent here", 2. "You sent to me"; *tašpurim* (the same, only f.); *tašpurānim* = 1. "you (pl.) sent here", 2. "you (pl.) sent to me". The remaining dative suffixes are usually joined to the ventive form of the verb with the final *m* of the ventive becoming assimilated to the first consonant of the suffix (§ 18d), e.g. *ašapparakkum* "I send to you" from **ašappar-am-kum*; *lillikakkim* "may he come to you (f.)" from **lillik* (§ 75c) + *-am-* + *kim*. But sometimes, especially in OB, the ventive endings are missing, e.g. *liddikkum* (§ 16b) "may he give to you (m. sg.)" from **lindin-kum*. In Mari and in OA only the 2nd person dative suffixes are attached to the ventive form, the 1st pl. and 3rd person sg. and pl. dative suffixes on the contrary being attached to the endingless verb form, e.g. *išpurniāti* (OA) "he wrote to us", *nutâršum* "we give back to him".

c The accusative suffixes are usually attached directly to the verb in question, e.g. *lîballiṭū-ka* "may they preserve your life", similarly *lîballiṭ-ka, lîballiṭū-kināti*, OA *iṣbatū-šunu* "they seized them". The 1 sg. acc. suffix in Bab. is joined to the ventive ending. The resulting forms are *-anni, -inni* (2 f. sg.) *-ūninni* (3 m. pl.) *-āninni* (3 f. pl.), e.g. *iṣbat-anni* "he seized me" (Ass. *iṣbat-ni*, OA also has *iṣbatī,* see § 26c under 4a), *ṭuppum ikšudanni* (Mari) "the tablet reached me";

ikkalūninni "they will devour me", *ibqurūninni* "they make good their claim against me" (acc. of pers.). In later times -*ūninni* and -*āninni* were dissimilated to -*ū'inni* and -*ā'inni*.

With endingless forms, if the final consonant is a dental (*d, t, ṭ*) or a sibilant (*z, s, ṣ, š*), it will combine with the *š* of the suffix to become *ss* (cf. § 20e), e.g. *ikšussu* "it reached him" from **ikšud-šu*; *iṣbassināti* "he seized them (f. pl.)" from **iṣbat-šināti*. Final *n* will assimilate to *k* and *š* to become *kk* and *šš*, e.g. *iddiššunūti* "he gave them" from **indin-šunūti*. **d**

If the verb has two suffixes, the dative precedes the accusative, e.g. *aṭrudakkuššu* "I sent him to you"; *ēzibakkuššu* "he left him to you" from **ēzib* (§ 75h) + *am* + *kum* + *šu*; *litrûnikkuššunūti* "may they lead them to you" from **litrû* + *nim* + *kum* + *šunūti*. The -*m* of the dative suffix assimilates to the following consonants. **e**

Final long vowels that have been shortened (§ 83a) reappear as long vowels before suffixes, e.g. *lîšebbi* (D stem of *šebûm* "to be satisfied"), but *lîšebbīka* "may he satisfy you" (cf. also § 8). **f**

E. PARTICLES (§§ 88-99)

1. Prepositions **88**

All prepositions govern the genitive (for *ana* see sect. b). **a**

1. True prepositions are: **b**

a) *ina* (older *in*) "in, on," in OA often assimilated to the following word, e.g. *i(n)šamši* = *iššamši* "on the day in which" (see §§ 41e and 115d). Beside its locative meaning there is also the temporal: "at the time"; the partitive: "among"; the causative: "because of"; and the instrumental: "by means of".

b) *ana* "to, toward", serves especially to express the dative, often being associated with dative forms of the independent pronoun (§ 25c) (cf. above sub a), e.g. *ana kâšim* "to you", *ana šuāšim* "to him", etc.; also with assimilation *akkâšim* (§ 25a). Assimilation of the proclitic *an* to a following consonant occurs particularly frequently in OA, e.g. *aṣṣēr* "to" (locative), "over and above, that"; *appūḫ* "instead of". Additional meanings are the temporal: "until, from, within"; the causative "because of"; purpose "for the purpose of" (often before an inf. "in order to", with the negative *ana lā* "in order not to", § 109fα).

c) *ištu* (later Bab. *ultu,* later Ass. *iltu, issu)* "from, out of"; temporal "since, after" (cf. § 115e).

d) *adi* "up ... to" (temporal and locative), "besides", rarely "during" (cf. § 115d).

e) *kī, kīma* "like, as" (cf. OA *kīma kuāti* "your representative"); *kīmū,* later *kūm* "instead of".

f) *ela* "except", not connected to pronominal suffixes.

g) *lāma* (cf. § 115a), later *lām* "before" (temporal); *ēma* (cf. § 94b) "wherever, to whatever".

c 2. The most significant derived prepositions are:

a) *eli* "upon, over, against". As a substantive it may be joined to a pronominal suffix (§ 26b): *elī-šu* "upon him".

b) *itti* (originally *ittum* "side") "with", Ass. *išti*. With a pronominal suffix *ittī-ya* "with me".

c) *balu(m)* (locative-adverbial, cf. § 90c) "without".

d) *aššu(m)* "on account of, for the sake of" (from *an(a)-šum)*, OA *aššumi* "regarding", cf. also § 94e.

e) *ašar* (originally *ašrum* "place") "where, whither" cf. § 94a.

f) *mala* (originally "abundance") = Ass. *ammar* "as many as, as much as, equally" see § 33).

2. Prepositional Expressions 89

Prepositional expressions were originally substantives, which are used with adverbial endings or in combination with prepositions. a

With adverbial endings are such examples as *elēn(um), elān(um)* "above" (also with suffixes *el*$^{\bar{e}}$*/ānukka* "beside you", etc.); *šaplān(um)* "below" (cf. on this § 90d).

Original substantives are combined with real prepositions to give a specific nuance, e.g. from *libbum* "heart": *ina libbi* (OA *illibbi*) "within, inside"; from *qerbum* "interior": *ana qereb* "to the midst of", *ina qereb* "in the midst of", *ultu qereb* "out of the midst of"; OA *iqqabli* (cf. § 41c) "in the midst of, in the course of (temp.)"; from *šaplum* "under side": *ina šapal* "below".

Other important prepositional expressions are: b

pānum "face, before": *ina pān* later Aramaicized *lapān*; *maḫar* ("front") "before"; *(w)arki* ("back") "behind, after"; *pūtum* ("front") "opposite", with prep. *ina pūt*; *ina meḫret* (*meḫertum* "front") "opposite"; *muḫḫum* "top of skull", only with the prep. *ina muḫḫi* "to the debit of" = *eli*, OA *ina ṣēr* (*iṣṣer* "on the back of"); *ina birīt* (originally "the intervening space") "between" (NA *bīt,* cf. § 19b); *ṭeḫi* (lit. "proximity") "adjoining", NB/LB *ṭēḫ, ṭāḫ*.

The following appear only in combination with true prepositions: *tarṣu* ("direction"): *ana tarṣi* "towards" (temp.); *ina tarṣi* "at the time of"; *ištu tarṣi* "from the time of"; *ana irat* (*irtum* "breast") "against, contrary to", etc. With *kī*: *kī pī* (*pûm* "mouth") "corresponding to, according to".

3. The Adverb (§§ 90-93).

90 *a. Adverbial Endings*

The most important adverbial endings to be noted are:

a 1. the acc. ending *-a(m)* (§ 39b), which principally forms adverbs of time and place, e.g. *ūma(m)* "in the daytime", *urra(m)* "tomorrow", *mūša(m)* "at night", *imitta(m)* "on the right", *šumēla(m)* "on the left". Also without mimation are: *warka* "later", *mišla* (OA) "by half";

b 2. the ending *-â* < *ia*, e.g. *aḫannâ* "every man for himself", *aḫullâ* "beyond", (from *aḫu* "shore" + *ullû* "other");

c 3. the locative ending *-um* (see § 44), e.g. *apputtum* (OA) "please", *balu(m)* "without", *qādum* "together with";

d 4. the suffix *-ānu(m)* principally forms adverbs of place and time: *elē*/*ānum* (§ 5a) "above", *šaplānum* (see § 89a) "below", *(w)arkānum* "later", OA *annânum* "from here", *ammânum* "from there" (cf. § 29d). With suffix *allânukka* "besides you";

e 5. the terminative ending *-iš* (see § 45), e.g. *eliš* "above", *šapliš* "below", *ašariš* "there, thence", *ēṣiš* (OA) "as soon as possible". An irregular form is *aḫāmiš* "one another" (cf. 93b). Cf. also *-iš-um*, e.g. *miššum* (OAkk, OA) "why?" SB *minsu*;[91]

f 6. the later suffix *-āniš* (cf. § 45c) forms adverbs of place, e.g. *elāniš* "above", *šaplāniš* "beneath";

g 7. the ending *-išam* (§ 45e) forms distributive adverbs, such as *(w)arḫišam* "monthly", *šattišam* "yearly, annually";

8. *-aš,* (later) infrequently used like *-iš*, e.g. *aḫrâtaš* (SB) "in the future"; **h**

9. *-atta(m), -atti* are used similarly to *-iš*, cf. *emuqattam* (OA) "forcibly". **i**

10. *-ī* serves for the formation of multiplicatives (cf. § 50) as e.g. *šiššī-šu* "sixfold", as well as for adverbs of time and place, e.g. *warki* "behind"; Ass. has *ē* as well as *ī: alê* (OA) "where?"; **j**

11. *-kīam* (OB) *-kam* (OA) forms advs. of place, e.g. *ayyikīam* (cf. § 91a), *ayyakam* (cf. § 31b) "where?", *ašrakam* "there", Bab. *ullīkī'am* (cf. § 29d), Ass. *ammakam* "there", *annakam* "here". **k**

b. Adverbs of Place 91

1. Interrogative adverbs: *ayyikīʾam* (see § 90k), later *ēkâ* "where?"; *ayyānum* (§ 86b) "where?", also with suffixes *ayyānuššu* "where is he?" **a**

2. For the adverbs such as *elēnum, šaplānum*; *eliš, šapliš, elāniš, šaplāniš* see § 90d-f above. **b**

c. Adverbs of Time 92

1. Interrogative adverbs: *mati* "when?", *adi mati* "how long?" **a**

2. *inanna,* later *enenna* "now"; *anumma* "now, at this point" (cf. § 57a); *inūmīšūma* "at that time"; *warkānu(m)* later *arki* (cf. § 94c) "after that, later", *ultu ulla* "for a long time". **b**

d. Modal and Causal Adverbs 93

1. Interrogative adverbs: *kī* "how?"; *ana mīnim* > *ammīn(m)* "why? wherefore?". **a**

b 2. *ki'am, kâm,* MB *akanna* "thus"; *ištēniš* "together"; *aḫāmiš* (§ 90e) "one another, mutually, reciprocally"; *mitḫāriš* "equally, in the same way", etc.

94 4. Subordinating Conjunctions

a In Akkadian prepositions (§ 88) or adverbial accusatives (§ 89a) can serve as subordinating conjunctions. The predicate of the dependent clause stands in the subjunctive (§ 59c).

b 1. Local: *ašar* (constr. st. of *ašrum* "place") "where? whither?" (cf. § 88c), *ēma* (only in Bab.) "where?" (cf. § 116).

c 2. Temporal: *inūma, enūma*, OAkk *inu(m)* "when", (cf. § 115b), *inūmi* "on the day when"; *ištu/ultu* (cf. § 88b) "as soon as, after" (cf. § 115e), *warki/a* (only in Bab.) "after" (also *arki ša), adi* "until" (cf. § 115d), "that", *lāma* "before", *kīma, kī* "as, when" (§ 115c).

d 3. Modal: *kīma, kī* "as, like", later *a(k)kī*, also *a(k)kī ša* "as soon as".

e 4. Causal (cf. § 117) *aššu(m)* "because" (see also § 88c).

95 5. Introductory and Modal Particles

a *šumma* "if" serves to introduce conditional sentences (see § 112). It also acts as a preposition, e.g. *šumma libbīka* "If you will". Direct address is introduced by *umma* "thus (says)" (esp. at the beginning of letters), instead of which in MA/NA *mā*. The optative (or "wish") particle is *lū* (see § 60a). In the older language (particularly OA) clause initial *mā* "what?" or "how?" was used to introduce direct speech.[92]

b Modal particles: *assurri* (OB and OA) "certainly, surely".[93]

6. Enclitic Particles 96

1. *-ma* (§ 100b) serves to join two sentences together (= "and then") or it can be used to emphasize a word. For the formation of indefinite relatives through attachment of *-ma* see § 33.

2. *-mi* to indicate quoted speech.

3. *-ni* as a subjunctive suffix in Ass.; in OAkk *-na* indicates dependent clauses (§ 59d).

4. *-man* (OA *-min*) introduces a contrary-to-fact clause, often dependent upon *šumma* (cf. § 112e note 2).

7. Conjunctions 97

Individual words or sentences are joined by conjunctions (see also *-ma* § 96 sub 1). The following are used as conjunctions.

a) *u* "and, also" (asyndeton is frequent).

b) For "either X or Y": X *ū* Y; X *lū* Y; X *ū lū* Y; *lū* X *lū* Y; *lū* X *ū lū* Y; *ū lū* X *ū lū* Y. Instead of *ū lū* Bab. can use *ūlu*, OB and OA can use *ul*, OA can use *ūla*. In negated sentences these are translated "neither … nor".

8. Negative Particles 98

1. *lā* "not" as a negation in subordinate clauses, questions and prohibitions (§§ 55b, 60e, 68e), occasionally in declarative sentences, especially frequent in Ass., e.g. *lā agammar* (OA) "I will not give up". The *lā* may be used proclitically to negate single words: *dabāb lā kitti* (§§ 103d and 109g) "untrue speech". a

2. *ul* (Bab.), *ulā* (older OB and OA) negate independent declarative sentences. b

c 3. *ai* (before a vowel), *ē* (before a consonant) are used as vetitive particles (cf. § 60d).

99 9. Interjections

a *i, e,* "ah!, well!", *kēna* "to be sure", *(a)gana* "come now", *enna(m)* "behold" (OA *amma), ūʾa* (exclamation) "alas!".

b Cf. also *i* with the cohortative (in Bab.): *i nillik* "come, let us go!" (cf. § 60c).

III. SYNTAX (§ 100-119)

A. THE SENTENCE AND ITS PARTS (§ 100-107)

1. The Simple Sentence 100

a In Akkadian there are two kinds of sentences: nominal and verbal.

b 1. Nominal sentences are those whose the predicate is a noun or pronoun. They can also be construed as negative (e.g., *ul abī attā* "you are not my father"), or as interrogative sentences (e.g., *ali kaspum,* "where is the money?"). Akkadian does not have helping verbs as copulas. However, the enclitic particle *-ma* (§ 96) often takes the place of a copula, e.g. *umma* PN-*ma* "so (says) PN" (cf. § 95) or the anaphoric pronoun *šū* (§ 25a).

c 2. Verbal sentences are those whose predicate is a finite verb, including the stative, e.g. *mārū ṣeḫḫerū* "the children were/are/will be small". With transitive verbs verbal sentences consist of subject, object and predicate.

Under the influence of Sumerian sentence structure the predicate stands at the end of the sentence (§ 1a), as in *ālam akšud* "I conquered the city". As a rule the object follows the subject, resulting in the following word order: subject, object, predicate, e.g. *šarrum ālam ikšud* "the king conquered the city". The predicate can stand first for emphasis, e.g. *uška*ʾʾ*in ana ṭuppim ša dīn kārim* (OA) "I have bowed to the tablet of the judgment of the colony." In poetry the predicate often stands at the beginning or in the middle of the sentence, e.g. *ikšuda būlu* (SB) "the wild animals came", *ātamar šanīta šutta* (SB) "I saw a second dream".

Such predicates as objects of prepositions and adverbs also precede the verb (numerous exceptions in poetry).

d 3. Compound nominal sentences are those whose predicate consists of an entire nominal or verbal phrase, e.g.

awīlum šū	*šību-šu*	*qerbū*
that man	his witnesses	are close by
Subject	Subject	Predicate

Complex clauses such as these differ from clauses like *šību awīlim šuāti ul qerbū* "The witnesses of that man are not close by" in that special emphasis is laid on the subject of the compound sentence. It is often possible to translate "as far as that man is concerned, his witnesses are not close by".

e Subject and predicate usually agree in gender and number. After collectives the plural is commonly used, e.g. *ṣābum ikšudūnim* "the people arrived". On the other hand, in Akkadian theophoric personal names the rules of gender agreement between subject and predicate do not always apply, e.g. *Ištar-pālil* (OA PN) "Ishtar (is) a keeper/guard".[94]

101 2. Attributives

a The attributive, by which a noun is more nearly defined, can be an adjective, verbal noun (participle) or an ordinal number.

b The attributive adjective agrees in gender, number and case with its related noun: *šarrum dannum* "the strong king", *šarratum dannatum* "the strong queen". The adjective only precedes its governing noun when it is particularly stressed, e.g. *kabtu nīr bēlūtī-ya* "the heavy yoke of my lordship". In the same way, ordinal numbers precede the noun to which they belong: *ina ḫamšim ūmim* "on the fifth day".

The attributive of a dual stands in the plural, e.g. *idān paglāti(m)* "mighty arms, powerful weapons", but in older periods (OAkk, OA) in the dual (cf. § 38c), e.g. *šenēn patītēn* "2 open shoes". With collectives the attributive can be sg. or pl., thus *ṣābum mādum* or *ṣābum mādūtum* "many people". **c**

When an attributive modifies two or more substantives it usually follows the last, and if the substantives are of different genders, it takes the masculine form: *lū wardam lū amtam ḫalqam* (OB) "either a male or a female escaped slave"; *mātāte u ḫuršāne dannūte* (NA) "mighty lands and mountains". **d**

Note: In the same way a single verb having multiple subjects agrees with the masculine, e.g. *mutum u aššutum ittaprusū* (OA) "the man and the wife have separated".

3. Apposition **102**

Words in apposition agree in number and case with their antecedent: *bīt ^{d}Anim u ^{d}Adad ilāni rabûti bēlēya* "the house of Anu and Adad, the great gods, my lords". If there is a genitive noun depending upon the word in apposition, the latter is singular (cf. also § 108b) *mārī nabnīt libbī-šu* (MB) "the sons, the offspring of his body" = "his biological sons"; *ālāni bīt dūrāni* (SB) "the cities, place(s) of walls" = "fortified places". **a**

Common uses of apposition are: **b**

1. to indicate material, e.g. *kilīlum kaspum* "a silver crown".

2. to indicate amounts, e.g. *10 mana* (absolute state, § 43a) *kaspum* "10 minas of silver"; *ina 3 naruq aršātim* (OA) "in the 3 sacks of barley".

c The substantives that signify the whole, totality, all, etc. (cf. § 34) and serve to express the English adjectives "all", "whole", "every", particularly *kalûm, kullatum, gimrum, napḫarum, seḫertum,* later *gabbu,* frequently follow the antecedent as appositional words, usually in combination with a resumptive pronoun. This is especially true of *kalûm* and *gabbu,* e.g. *mušīta kalâ-ša* "the whole night"; *tamirtu gabbī-ša* (MB) "the whole field"; *mātāt nakirī kalî-šin* "the lands of the enemies, (namely) their totality" = "all the enemy lands".

103 4. Genitive

a The genitive (§ 39) always follows its governing noun, which is in the construct state (§ 41), e.g. *bīt awīlim* " the house of the citizen". The gen. defines the noun more precisely, e.g. *pet* (from *petû,* cf. § 41h) *uznim* "open with respect to the ear," i.e., "open eared" (= intelligent). It can also be used to express belonging, e.g. *māt Šumerim u Akkadîm* (OB) "the land of Sumer and Akkad", *erṣet Sippar* "the territory of Sippar".

b Construct chains can fuse almost to a single word, e.g. *bēl ḫubullim* "lord of the interest" = "creditor", *bēl salīmim* "friend", *āl šarrūtim* "royal city". Suffixes can only be attached to the final member of the construction: *bēl salīmī-ki* "your friend", *āl šarrūtī-šu* "his royal city".

c Attributives of the construct (first member) must follow the genitive (final member), cf. *šar mātātim dannum* "the mighty king of the lands".

d The dependent genitive cannot be separated from the word it modifies. The exception is the negative *lā* (§ 98a and 109g), e.g. *awāt lā kittim* (OB) "an untrue word", lit. "a word of untruth"; *bēl lā ilim* (OA) "irreligious person".

For the infinitive with the negative see under inf. § 109g. e

5. Genitive Formations with *ša* 104

a Instead of a construct chain one may also use a formation with *ša* (§ 30a). This is necessary when the genitive is separated from its governing noun by an attributive, e.g. *zērum dārium ša šarrūtim* (OB) "eternal seed of kingship"; *šarrum dannum ša mātātim* "mighty king of the lands (equivalent to *šar mātātim dannum*, see § 103f), or if two genitives depend upon the same substantive, as for example *bilat eqlim ša šanātim* (OB) "the produce of the fields for the years", or if one genitive depends upon two substantives, e.g. *alpū u immerātum ša ekallim* (Mari) "the oxen and sheep of the palace".

Note: Rarely *ša* plus genitive is used without antecedent, e.g. *ana ša Nibas* (OA) "for the (festival) of Nibas" (cf. § 30).

b Sometimes the genitive with *ša* will stand before the antecedent (especially in poetry), in which case the genitive will be re-expressed by a resumptive pronoun: *ša Tiāmat karassa* (SB) "the mood of Tiamat"; *ša M. aštakan dabdâšu* "of M., I brought about his defeat".

c The frequent appearance of an anticipatory pronoun before the genitive with *ša* in LB is an Aramaism, e.g. *A. māršu (marʾūšu) ša B.* "A. (his) son of B" (it occasionally appears, however, already in OB, cf. *šumša ša ṣuḫartim* "the name of the maiden").

For the genitive of the infinitive with *ša* see under inf. § 109g.

105 **6. Accusative**

a The object of transitive verbs is in the accusative case, e.g. *ālam akšud* "I conquered the city". Many times intransitive verbs are construed with the acc. (the so-called accusative of the way), although the acc. has not actually been acted upon, e.g. *ḫarrānam ittalak* "he has gone on a (business) trip"; *irappud ṣēra* (SB) "he roams the steppe"; *ḫarrāna illik* (SB) "he went on the way"; *šadâšu ēmid* (MB/LB) "he took refuge on his mountain", i.e., "he disappeared".

The acc. is used:

b a) to specify location in answer to the question "where?" It is especially frequent in OA, e.g. *eqlam wašbāni* "we sat in the field"; *bāb ilim ubbib-šu* "he purified him at the gate of the god". For adverbs of place, as for example *imittam u šumēlam* "on the right and left", cf. §90a.

c b) to specify time in answer to the questions "when?" and "how long?", e.g. *mūšī u urrī* "during the nights and the days" = "day and night", *urram u šērām* (in Mari also with the prep. *ana)* "in the future".

d c) to specify a point of reference: *mê iṭīb libbašu* (SB) "his heart rejoiced at the water"; *igpuš libbu* (SB) "he became massive with respect to the heart" = "he became overbearing". Especially with the 1st person sg. suff., e.g. *imqut-anni* "It fell down (with reference to) me"; *ittallak-niāti* (OB) "he has gone away (with reference to) us".[95]

e d) To express condition with abstracts ending in *–ūtum,* e.g. *rēqūs-su* (from the abstract *rēqūtū*) "with empty hands"; *balṭūssu ikšudūšu* "they seized him in his living state (i.e., "while he was alive"). In OA, similar to the Arabic *ḥāl*-acc.

(also formed with adjectives): *šalmam u kēnam išaqqal* (OA) "he shall weigh (it) out in sound and stable condition".

Note: Examples of a frozen accusative of condition with a following genitive are: *rapšam uznim* "of wide understanding", or *atram-ḫasīs*, "of extreme cleverness".[96] f

7. Double Accusative Formations 106

Double accusatives appear with:

1. causative stems, if the verb is transitive in the G-stem, e.g. *eqlam ṣēnī* (pl. acc.) *uštākil* "he caused the sheep to graze in the field", *ṭuppam ušašmēka* (OA) "I read the tablet to you" (lit. "I caused you to hear the tablet"). a

2. various verbs, such as "to water, give to drink" (*šaqûm*), "to load" (*ṣênum)*, "to fill (*mullûm*), "to name, call" (*nabûm*), "to place" (*nadûm*); so also *apālum* "to pay someone something", lit. "to satisfy someone with something", e.g. *kaspam ītaplanni* "he paid silver to me" *eṣēnši ḫurāṣu* (SB) " I loaded it (the ship) with gold".

When those verbs that take a double accusative appear in the passive, only the direct object appears in the nominative: *puluḫtam lū labšāti* (OB), "be (f. sg.) clothed with fear" (lit. "be one who has put fear on yourself"). b

8. Construction of Numbers 107

The numbers "1" (*ištēn*/*ištiat*) and "2" (*šina*/*šitta*) agree in gender with the thing being numbered, while with the numbers 3-10 forms in the absolute state in apposition are placed before the item; in fact, if the item is masculine, the number will be feminine and vice versa (the so-called Semitic polarity), e.g. *šalaš(a)t ūmī* "3 days", *samānē šanātim* "8 years". The number "4" is construed as a substantive in *kibrāt* a *arba ʾim* or *erbettim* "the four regions of the world". The numbers over 11 have only one form without gender distinction.

b The item numbered normally appears in the plural, but also sometimes in the singular, e.g. *ḫamiš ubānātim* (LB) "five fingers (long)", but *šalāšā ḫaṣbattum rēqtum* "thirty empty pots". The number "2" appeared with the dual in the older language (cf. § 38c), but later with the plural.

c The ordinal numbers usually precede the substantive, e.g. *ina šaluštim šattim* "in the third year"; but for greater emphasis, they follow, e.g. *aššatam šanītam lā eḫḫaz* (OA) "he shall not take a second wife", as contrasted with *ina šanîm ūmim* "on the second day".

B. Construction of the Verbal Nouns (§ 108-109)

108 **1. Participle**

a The participle may be construed as an adjective or a substantive. In the latter case it is connected as a noun to a dependent genitive, e.g. *ālik ḫarrānim* "traveler", *b/wābil* (cf. § 80f) *ṭuppim* "the bearer of the tablet". Participles avoid constructions with prepositions; cf., e.g. the divine epithets: *ᵈX āšib Y* "the god X who lives in (temple) Y"; or: *muštēmiqu ša ilti* (SB), "one who entreats the goddess".

b When a participle in the construct functions as an attributive to a plural substantive, it may appear in the singular form (see also § 41i and 101a): on the one hand, *ilāni ālikūt idīya* "the gods who go at my side"; on the other hand, *ardāni dāgil* (sg.!) *pānīya* "slaves who see my face".

c If a participle has two objects, the first takes the genitive and the second the accusative, cf. *mušalbiš warqim gigunê* *ᵈAyya* (OB), "the one who clothes the sanctuary of (the goddess) Ayya in green".

2. Infinitive[97] 109

a The Akkadian infinitive is a verbal noun, i.e., a substantive that can be construed verbally. As a substantive it is declined and can function in the clause as subject or object, or stand in the genitive following a preposition. Verbally, it often replaces a finite verb and can have a subject or object.

a. Nominal Construction b

A genitive can depend upon a substantival infinitive, e.g. *alāk gerrīya išme* (SB) "he heard of the course of my campaign"; *ana kašād māt nakrī* "for the conquest of the enemy land". The genitive, which in both previous cases indicates the object, can also express a subject, e.g. *ina šalām ḫarrānim* (OB) "when the journey is completed", *ina erāb annikim* (OA) "when the tin arrives". The genitive can also come between the preposition and the infinitive, e.g. *ina Šamaš napāḫi* (SB) "at sunrise".

b. Verbal Construction c

As a verb the infinitive can have a subject, e.g. *mussa ina muāte* (MA) "if her husband dies", or an object, e.g. *dannum enšam ana lā ḫabālim* (OB) "so that the strong may do no injustice to the weak". If the object comes between the preposition and the infinitive, it is put in the genitive, e.g. *ana kaspim šaqālim* "for the weighing out of silver".

d Paronomastic infinitive constructions. The infinitive serves to intensify verbal forms in the so-called paronomastic infinitive constructions. The infinitive stands in the locative-adverbial case in *–um* (§ 44e) with the enclitic *–ma* (§ 96), e.g.

šapārum-ma ašpur (OB) "I have certainly sent"; *ragāmum-ma ula iraggam* (OA) "he will certainly not raise any claim"; also without *–ma*, e.g. *erēšum errišū* "they will certainly sow"; *qâšu qīšam* (SB) "give me anyway".

e As subject the infinitive is usually construed nominally, e.g. *wašāb ugbabtim ul naṭu* "the dwelling of the hierodule is not desired"; similarly *wašābka īnam ul maḫir* (Mari) "your tarrying is not desired".

f Infinitive as object. Various verbs can have infinitives as acc.-object, so especially the verbs of ability (*leʾûm*, § 84j), volition (*mâʾum* OA, § 84k), commanding (*qabûm*) among others, e.g. *tadānam lā imūa* (OA) "he doesn't want to give"; *šaqālam qabi* "it was commanded him to count"; *ḫalāq ālīšu … liqbi* "let him command that his city be destroyed". In the old language *qabû* is also construed with the terminative-adverbial of the infinitive in *–iš* (see § 45a), e.g. *nadāniš qabi* "he was commanded to give".

g As genitive-attributive the infinitive can be appended to a noun, e.g. *aban alādi* (SB) "stone for giving birth"; *amāt ḫadê* "good news". In negative expressions the negation *lā* comes between construct and genitive (cf. § 98a and 103d), e.g. *arrat lā napšuri* "an unbreakable curse"; *erṣet lā târi* "land of no return" (= netherworld). The infinitive in the genitive following the determinative pronoun *ša* (§ 30) means "that of doing", "something to be done", e.g. *ša nadānim* "that of giving", i.e., "something to give".

h The infinitive with prepositions:

α 1. With most prepositions constructions can be formed, which stand for various kinds of dependent clauses and can completely replace them. With *ana* and *aššum* for final clauses: e.g. *ana lā ḫabālim* "that no injustice be done"; *aššum ina bītim šūṣîm* "that they be brought out of the house". The object dependent on the infinitive stands either in the acc. before a preposition, e.g. *raggam u ṣēnam ana ḫulluqim* "in order to destroy the bad and the evil", or if it follows the preposition, in the genitive. Thus constructions arise: *ana tarbītim nasāḫim* (OB) = *tarbītam ana nasāḫim* "to disinherit an adoptive child". In addition to from the verbal governance of the infinitive with the acc. object, nominal constructions of the infinitive with a following genitive occur also (usually in literary texts), e.g. *ana šutēšur nišī* (OB) "in order to rule the people justly".

2. The infinitive following *ina* represents temporal clauses, β
e.g. *ina ašāb bēlīya* "at the dwelling of my lord", i.e. "when my lord is/was present"; *ṭuppī ina amārīka* "when you read my tablet"; *ina bāb muātīšu* (OA) "when he was about to die". Also after other prepositions, such as *ištu, adi, kī(ma)*, e.g. *ṭuppī kīma šemêm* "when he (you) read(s) my letter"; *adi alākīya* "until I come".

3. In the temporal constructions the preposition (esp. in γ
Bab.) immediately precedes the infinitive: on the contrary *ina še᾿im leqêm ukannūšu* (OB) "they shall prove that he took the grain"; *kīma libbi* PN *lā marāṣim epuš* "act so, that PN may not be saddened".

C. Sentence Connectives (§§ 110-112)

1. Kinds of Sentence Connectives[98] 110

Clauses are connected by *–ma* (§ 96) "and". The conjunction *–ma* usually serves to join coordinate clauses, in order to express a logical, not just a temporal sequence. Since

Akkadian had not yet developed subordination everywhere, coordinate clauses replace many clause structures, such as, e.g. consecutive (§ 111) and conditional clauses (§ 112). Syntactic coordination displays a fixed sequence of tenses, by means of which notions of temporal sequence and logical connection are expressed.

111 **2. Tense Sequence**

a When temporal sequence is to be expressed by two clauses connected by *–ma*, past action can be expressed in the protasis by the preterite, but be continued in the apodosis by the perfect (§ 57), e.g. *īnūḫū-ma aṭṭardaššunūti* "after they had rested, I sent them on". This so-called t e n s e s e q u e n c e (Latin *consecutio temporum*) occurs only in OB and OA, since in the older language the perfect indicates just completed actions, e.g. *šumma dayyānum dīnam idīn … warkānum-ma dīnšu īteni* (OB) "if a judge renders a verdict … but later changes (lit. has changed) his verdict"; *nērub taḫsīsātim nītamar* (OA) "we entered and then saw the memoranda." The preterite stands here for the pluperfect, the perfect for simple past, e.g. *āpulšūma u ittalak* (Mari) "after I satisfied him, he departed".

b From MB on, after the perfect had become the form for affirmations about the past, in contrast to the preterite as the form for simple statements, there is no longer any observable tense sequence; cf. MB *iknuk ušēbila* "he sealed and sent" in contrast to OB *aknukam-ma uštēbilakkum* "I sealed and then sent it to you". Such clause connections are therefore expressed in the later language mostly by preterite + preterite.

3. Conditional Clauses 112

a Conditional clauses are rendered in Akkadian by main clauses, whose verb stands in the indicative. They occur sometimes as main clauses without an introductory particle. Clauses of this type are connected by *–ma*, e.g. *taša*ʾʾ*al-ma iqabbakku* (MB) "if you ask, he will tell you".

b Much more frequent are conditional clauses with introductory *šumma* (§ 95) "if". The preterite tense is employed in the protasis, e.g. *šumma awīlum kaspam ilqe* (OB) "if a citizen receives (lit. received) money". *lā* serves as the negation: *šumma awīlum aššatam lā īḫuz* "if a citizen didn't take the woman (in question) in marriage". For the tense sequence in OB conditional clauses see § 111a.

c In distinction to the preterite, which one uses for real conditional clauses, the perfect tense in the protasis has in OB a potential or hypothetical notion, e.g. *šumma lā iqtabi* "in the case that he has not said"; *šumma ina bītim ittaṣi* (Mari) "in case he should go out of the house".

d The present in the apodosis serves to indicate wishing to do or being obligated to do, e.g. *šumma awīlum ... ana maṣṣarūtim inaddin* (OB) "if a citizen ... wants to deposit (something) for safe-keeping"; *šumma ana Kaniš lā illak* (OA) "if he doesn't wish to travel to Kaniš"; *šumma uwaššar bēlī lišpuram* (Mari) "let my lord write me if I should release (them)".

e The stative in conditional clauses serves to indicate states, e.g. *šumma awīlum ina ḫarrānim wašib* (OB) "if a citizen finds himself on the road"; *šumma kasapšu watar* PN *ilaqqe* (OA) "if his silver is more than enough, PN will take (the excess)". Similarly in nominal sentences, e.g. *šumma ḫarrākka*

(= *ḫarrān-ka*, § 16b) *ana ālim* (OA) "if your road (leads) to the City".

Note 1: In NB/LB *šumma* is replaced by *kī*, whereby the verb as in temporal clauses stands in the subjunctive.

Note 2: Unreal clauses (cf. § 96,4) are formed by the particle *–man* (OB), *–min* (OA), which is appended to *šumma*, e.g. *šumma-min mētāku* (OA) "if I had died".

D. DEPENDENT CLAUSES (§§ 113-119)

113 1. Kinds of Dependent Clauses

In dependent clauses the verb stands in the subjunctive (§ 59c). According to their content, one distinguishes relative clauses (dependent on a pronoun or noun) and subordinate clauses (dependent on subordinating conjunctions). The subordinate clauses are subdivided according to their character into temporal clauses, causal clauses, etc.

114 2. Relative Clauses

a ***a) Relative clause with the determinative pronoun:***

α 1. In the older language the inflected determinative pronoun *šu* (§ 30b), soon to be replaced by the indeclinable *ša* (§ 30a), still occurs as a relative pronoun, for example, OB *šu iqīšu* "who gave", later *ša iqīšu*. The verb in the dependent clause stands in the subjunctive (§ 59c), to which in Ass. the particle *–ni* (§ 59d) is often suffixed, e.g. *kaspum ša* PN *ilqeʾuni* (OA) "silver that PN took".

β 2. When *ša* expresses the genitive or dative, it must be resumed in the relative clause by a corresponding pronominal suffix, e.g. gen.: *šarrūtum ša išdā-ša šuršudā* (OB) "a kingdom, (of which it is said that) its foundations are firm" = "a kingdom whose foundations are firm", or dative: *rēʾum ša* …

innadnūšum (OB) "a herdsman to whom (animals) have been given".

3. On the other hand, the pronominal suffix often is missing, when *ša* stands in the accusative, since *ša* in origin is an accusative of the determinative pronoun *šu* (§ 30b): *ṣēnū ša šarrum iddinu* (OB) "the small cattle (sheep and goats) that the king has given". But cf.: *ana* KUR*Uišdiš ša Ursa ēkimu-š(u) aqṭirib* (SB) "I approached the land of Uišdiš, which Ursa had taken (= had conquered)". γ

b) Relative clause without a pronoun: b

When the determinative pronoun *ša* is omitted, the noun on which the relative clause depends, appears in the construct (§ 41), even as the object, e.g. *awāt iqbû* (= *awātum ša iqbû*) "the word that he said (informal English: the word he said)"; *qīšti šarrum iddinu* "the gift that the king gave"; *bīt imqutu ippeš* "he is rebuilding the house that fell"; *ṭēm ešmû aštaprakkum* "I have sent to you the report that I heard".

Note: Relative clauses that without *ša* depend directly upon a noun in the construct, are almost unknown in OA.[99]

c) Nominal sentence as a relative clause. c

Nominal sentences, insofar as they represent relative clauses, are not outwardly distinguished in Bab. from main clauses, but in Ass. the subjunctive particle *–ni* (§ 59d and 96) is appended to the predicate, e.g. *ṭuppam ša werûm werī-ni ukâl* (OA) "I have a tablet (that proves) that the copper is my copper".

d) Relative clauses with generalizing pronouns: d

Even generalizing relatives (§ 33) can serve as relative pronouns, such as

1. the interrogative pronoun *mannum* (§ 31): *mannu ša* "whoever";

2. the indefinite pronoun *mamman* (OAkk and OA) "whoever", *mimma* (§ 32c) "whatever, everything that"; *luqūtam mamman iṣbutu* (OA) "whoever also seizes the wares"; *mimma kaspim ilqe'u* (OA) "whatever of silver he has taken". Cf. also *mimma šumšu* "whatever its name", i.e., "everything possible";

3. *mala* (construct state of the substantive *malû* "fullness, wealth, abundance", cf. § 88c), Ass. *(am)mar* with following relative clause "everything that", e.g. *mala ippaluka* (OB) "everything that he will answer you", *kaspam mala ilqe'u* (OA) "however much silver he has taken", *ammar šarru išpuranni* "everything that the king wrote to me" (the subjunctive suffix *–ni* in Ass. is appended to the ventive ending, cf. § 59d).

115 **3. Temporal Clauses**

a Temporal clauses are introduced by subordinating conjunctions (§ 94). Usually they precede the main clause. The tense in temporal clause and main clause is regulated according to the principles of tense sequence (§ 111). In Akkadian, temporal clauses are distinguished by the kind of subordinating conjunction employed in the temporal clause: with *inūma, kīma, ištu, adi, lama*, etc.

b ***a. Temporal Clauses with* inūma/i *(§ 94b) "when":***

α 1. When an action completed in the past is described, the verb usually stands in the preterite in both clauses, e.g.: *inūmi* PN *illikanni* … *kaspam ublam* (OA) "when PN came … he brought the silver".

2. When the antecedence of the action in the temporal clause is to be stressed, the perfect is followed by the present or a wish form in the sense of a futurum exactum, e.g. *inūma ittūram aššassu itabbal* (OB) "when he (the first husband) will have returned, he will take back his wife". β

3. When the coincidence of both actions in the present or future is to be expressed, both verbs stand in the present, e.g. *inūmi kaspam išaqqulu u ṣuḫāram itarru* (OA) "when he pays the silver, he will also get the child". γ

b. Temporal Clauses with **kīma** *(§ 94c) "as soon as":* c

1. With the preterite to express an action in the past, e.g. *kīma ṭuppi bēlīya illikam* (OB) "when my lord's letter arrived"; *kīma ṭuppam tašmeʾu alkam* (OA) "come as soon as you have read the tablet". α

2. For OB temporal clauses with *kīma,* the later dialects use *kī* with preterite in the dependent clause and perfect in the main clause, whereby *kī* usually stands immediately before the verb, e.g. *kī nilliku ana* PN *niqtabi* "as soon as we had come, we said to PN". β

3. *kīma* or *kī* (MB) with the perfect in the dependent clause and present or imperative in the main clause serves to express antecedence in a future clause, e.g. *kīma tattalkānim ṭēmam gamram šuprānim* "send (pl.) me a complete report as soon as you (pl.) have arrived". γ

c. Temporal Clauses with **adi** *(§ 94c) "until" and* **ūm** *"on the day that, when":* d

Temporal clauses with *adi* "until, as long as" usually have the present or stative in the dependent clause, e.g. *adi illakam* "until he arrives", *adi balṭu* "as long as he lives" (also *adi ūm balṭu*). After *ūm* "on the day that, when", OA *ina šamši* (*iššamši*, § 41c) the preterite or present, e.g. OB: *ūm ṭuppaka āmuru* "when I have read (lit. seen) your tablet"; OA: *ina šamši* PN *ūṣânni* "as soon as PN has gone forth"; *ina šamši našpertī tašamme'u* "when you (sg.) hear my message". Cf. also OAkk and OB date formulas: *in śanat Šar-kali-šarrī Amurram ikšudu* (OAkk) "in the year that Š. conquered the Amorites".

e **d. *Temporal Clauses with* ištu(m) *(SB* ultu*),* warka/i *"after" and* lāma *"before":***

α "After" is expressed with the subordinating conjunction *ištu* and (only Bab.) *warka/i* (cf. § 94c): 1. *ištu* (on this cf. § 88b) associates with the preterite, e.g. *ištum imūtu* (OAkk) "after he has died"; *ištu sinništum īrubu* (OB) "after the woman has entered"; *ištu ninnamru* "after we have seen each other" or the perfect (for indicating antecedence), e.g. *ištu* (= *warki*) *ilša iqterûši* (OB) "after her god has called her to himself" (= after she has died), or the present (to indicate the future), e.g. *ištū-ma tallakāni* "as soon as you (pl.) go" or with the stative, e.g. *ištu ina … wašbāku* "since I have been living in …"; *ištu riksū kankūni* (OA) "after the bands were sealed"; 2. *warka/i* with the preterite or the perfect, e.g. *warka abum ana šīmtim ittalku* (OB) "after the father has gone to his fate" (= has died). (Cf. also the example cited above sub 1.).

β The pret. stands after *lāma* "before" to designate the past, e.g. *lāma illikūninni … maṣṣartam ipte'ū* (OA) "before they came here … (the sons of PN) opened the storeroom".

4. Local Clauses 116

ašar (§ 94b) "where?, whither?", *ali* "where?" or (only in Bab.) *ēma* (§ 49b) "wherever" are used as subordinating conjunctions, e.g. *ašar illiku* "where he has gone"; *ašar kaspum ibaššiu leqe* (OA) "where silver exists, take (it)"; *ašar damqat-ni neppaš* (OA) "we will trade wherever it is good"; *ali ammurušu kaspī alaqqe* (OA) "wherever I see him, I will take my money (lit. silver)"; *ēma allaku* "where I also go"; *ēma elīša ṭābu* "where she prefers (lit. where it is good to her)".

5. Causal Clauses 117

aššu(m) (§ 94e) "because" is used as the subordinating conjunction, e.g. *aššum uldu* (OB) "because she has given birth". Also in the sense "so that" (OA *aššumi*): *aššum... lā išebbirū* "so that they do not smash ..."; *aššumi têrtī u anāku errabanni* (OA) "so that my instructions and I may arrive". *ištū-ma* "since indeed", "because" is also used in the causal sense, and at times (in the later language) even *kī*.

6. "That" Clauses 118

"That" clauses (so-called object clauses) in the older language are introduced by *kīma*, e.g. *ul tīde kīma elānukki aḫātam lā īšû* (OB) "Don't you know that I have no sister other than you?"; *lā tīdeʾā kīma maknakam ipteʾū* (OA) "Don't you (pl.) know that he has opened the sealed room?" In the later language *kī* (cf. § 115cγ) replaces *kīma*.

7. Oaths 119

Oaths are often indicated by the subjunctive, e.g. *ana ili telqû* (OB) "you (sg.) took by means of a god('s oath)"; *mimma lā alqeʾu* (OA) "I most certainly did not take anything", or by a conditional clause (protasis) without an apodosis, whereby in Ass. the verb stands in the subjunctive.[100] Positive and negative assertions are interchanged: *šumma mimma kaspam ilqeʾu* "He certainly took no silver" (actually: "If he has taken any silver, [then let such-and-such happen]"); *šumma lā iqbianni* "He certainly did say to me".

Endnotes

[1] See also I. J. Gelb, "Notes on von Soden's Grammar of Akkadian", BiOr XII (1955), 96ff.

[2] Issued in a second, revised and expanded edition (1961).

[3] Just as in the recently appeared "Grammatica della lingua Accadica" (Analecta Hierosolymitana 1, 1962) by A. Lancellotti and "Akkadskij jazyk" (Moscow 1964) by L. A. Lipin. (In contrast the "literary dialect [SB]" forms the basis of E. Reiner's structural grammar "A Linguistic Analysis of Akkadian" [1966].)

[4] Especially the reviews of J. A. Brinkman, BiOr 23 (1966), 293ff., K. Deller, Or NS 34 (1965), 79ff. and J. Oelsner, OLZ 1969 (in press) [translator's note: see now OLZ 64 (1969) 33-35].

[5] Cf. on this W. von Soden, "Zur Einteilung der semitischen Sprachen," WZKM 56 (1960), 177-191.

[6] Detailed treatment by A. Finet, L'accadien des lettres de Mari (1956), reviewed by Gelb in Language 33 (1957), 197-208.

[7] A comprehensive grammar of Old Assyrian is being prepared by K. Hecker. [Translator's note: Now published as Grammatik der Kültepe Texte (AnOr 44, Rome 1968).]

[8] J. Aro, Studien zur Mittelbabylonischen Grammatik (SO XX, 1955).

[9] According to J. P. Hyatt, The Treatment of Final Vowels in Early Neo-Babylonian (1941), NB begins at the end of the Kassite period.

[10] K. Deller, "Zur sprachliche Einordnung der Inschriften Aššurnaṣirpals II", Or NS 26 (1957), 144-156.

[11] A comprehensive grammar of Neo-Assyrian is planned by K. Deller.

[12]Cf. now E. Salonen, Untersuchungen zur Schrift und Sprache des Altbabylonischen von Susa (SO XXVII/1, 1962) and L. de Meyer, L'accadien des contrats de Suse (1962).

[13]In addition to the abbreviations employed here, as well as in GAG and AHw, for the individual Akkadian dialects, we have added (in parentheses) also the English designations used in the CAD: aAK (OAkk) — aB (OB) — mB (MB) — jB (SB) — nB (NB) — spB (LB) — aA (OA) — mA (MA) — nA (NA). (Translator's note: So read Matouš's footnote. For this English edition we have substituted the CAD abbreviations in all cases.)

[14] Bisyllabic values of the type *baba*, partly already in Sumerian and in the oldest Akkadian linguistic levels, were developed in greater scope in the Neo-Assyrian period.

[15]For the concept "logogram" cf. A. Falkenstein, Archäische Texte aus Uruk (1936), 29ff.

[16]I. J. Gelb, "WA = *aw, iw, uw* in Cuneiform Writing," JNES 20 (1961), 194-196.

[17]E. Reiner, "Phonological Interpretation of a Subsystem," St. Op. 179f.

[18]Cf. K. Deller, "Studien zur neuassyrischen Orthographie," Or NS 31 (1962), 194-196.

[19]A complete list of determinatives is in AHw VII.

[20]For the designation of length in the writing see J. Aro, Abnormal plene Writings in Akkadian Texts (SO XIX/11, 1953).

[21]See now E. Sollberger, "Graeco-babylonica", Iraq 24 (1962), 63-72 and W. Röllig "Griechische Eigennamen in Texten der babylonischen Spätzeit", Or NS 29 (1960), 376-391.

[22] On this K. Deller, Lautlehre des Neuassyrischen (Dissertation), § 22.

[23]Probably not under Sumerian influence. Cf. West Semitic borrowing *hkl* (Ugar., Phoen., Old Aram.) from Sumerian é . g a l "palace". On this E. Sollberger, AfO 17 (1954-56), 11 note 4 and E. E. Knudsen, DLZ 87 (1966), 685f.

[24]See on this I. J. Gelb, MAD II^{2} 88f.

[25]Cf. K. Deller, Diss. §23 and AHw 238.

[26]See on this AHw s.v. (communication of W. von Soden) and K. Hecker, AnOr 44 (1968) § 10 c.

[27]Cf. K. Deller, Diss. §26.

[28]See on this K. Hecker, AnOr 44 (1968) § 32 b, and L. Matouš-K. Petráček, "Beiträge zur akkadischen Grammatik" in ArOr 24 (1956), 1-14.

[29]According to AHw 328a *ḫarrumum* pl. to *ḫarmum.*

[30]See on this K. Deller, Or NS 31 (1962), 194-196.

[31]On the semi-vowels *w* and *y* cf. E. Reiner, St.Op. 173-180.

[32]See on this I. J. Gelb, MAD II^2 25.

[33]K. Deller, Diss. §26.

[34]Cf. K. Deller, Diss. §47.

[35]For MB examples see J. Aro, Studien, 38-40.

[36]Further examples in K. Hecker, AnOr 44 (1968) § 35 b.

[37]Cf. K. Deller, Diss. §41, and J. J. Finkelstein, "Akkadian *bīt*: *bi(r)t* = WS *beyt*: *bey(na)t*", JNES 21 (1962), 90-92.

[38]Cf. on this W. von Soden, "Akkadisch *abarša* und der sumerische Laut *r*", WZKM 55 (1959), 51-53, and R. Borger, "Zur Aussprache des Gottesnamens Ninurta," Or NS 30 (1961), 203.

[39]Cf. A. Goetze, "The Sibilants of Old Babylonian," RA 52 (1958), 137-149 and J. Aro, "Die semitischen Zischlaute (*th*), *š, ś* und ihre Vertretung im Akkadischen," Or NS 28 (1959), 321-335.

[40]On this M. Held, "*mḫṣ*/ *mḫš* in Ugaritic and other Semitic Languages," JAOS 79 (1959), 169-176 (esp. 173).

[41]On this K. Deller, Diss. §46h.

[42]E. E. Knudsen, "Cases of Free Variants in the Akkadian *q* Phoneme," JCS 15 (1961), 84-90. For Mari see A. Finet, L'accadien, §12d.

[43]For explanation cf. Fr. R. Kraus, RSO XXXII (1957), 103-108.

[44]Cf. on this M. Held, JCS 15 (1961), 3 note 22.

[45]Cf. B. Landsberger, ZA 41 (1933), 232f. and R. Borger, Asarhaddon, 68 note 15.

[46]Cf. K. Deller, Diss. §27f and §28a/b.

[47]Cf. W. von Soden, "Akkadisch", Linguistica Semitica Presente e future (1961), 39.

[48]Cf. on this G. Dossin, Syria 32 (1955), 27f. and B. Landsberger–K. Balkan, Belleten 14 (1950), 248ff.

[49]Cf. in detail GAG §§54-56.

[50]The root **prs* serves as paradigm. Obviously only a limited number of the forms adduced here are attested for each root.

[51]Cf. on this most recently W. von Soden–W. Röllig, Das akkadische Syllabar (2. ed. 1967), p. XXIII.

[52]On the origin of the ending *-ūt* compare L. Gulkowitsch, Die Bildung von Abstraktbegriffen in der hebräischen Sprachgeschichte, 128-132.

[53]Cf. A. Falkenstein, ZA 42 (1934), 152-154.

[54]For the fem. ending cf. I.J. Gelb, BiOr 12 (1955), 106f.

[55]According to I. J. Gelb, Language 33 (1957), 202 and R. Borger, BAL §§63i, 64 l-n instead of *-ānu* it is perhaps better to read *-ānū*, and instead of *-āni* (cf. below §39e) accordingly *-ānī*.

[56]For Mari see A. Finet, L'accadien, §26n, for OA see K. Balkan, Letter of King Anum-Ḫirbi, 20.

[57]Or *-ānū/ī*? Cf. above §38e note 55.

[58]Cf. on this A. Finet, L'accadien, §26b.

[59]On this A. Falkenstein, Das Sumerische, 15 and MAD III 263.

[60]I. J. Gelb, MAD II^2 146.

[61]Cf. K. Hecker, AnOr 44 (1968) § 62 b and AHw 427a.

[62]Cf. K. Deller, Diss. §37e.

[63]W. von Soden, "Die Zahlen 20-90 im Semitischen und der Status absolutus", WZKM 57 (1961), 24-28.

[64]Cf. I. J. Gelb, RA 50 (1956) 4f.

[65]See on this above §43a note 63.

[66]Also called the Permansive. Cf. M. B. Rowton, "The Use of the Permansive in Classic Babylonian" in JNES 21 (1962), 233-303.

[67]Cf. M. B. Rowton, l. c. 239.

[68]Cf. on this W. von Soden, "Das akkadische *t*-Perfekt und sumerische Verbalformen mit *ba-, imma-* und *u-*" in AS 16, 103-110.

[69]For MB cf. J. Aro, Studien, 80ff.

[70]Translator's note: Ungnad-Matouš used the opposition of German *her* and *hin*. In English we do not usually employ "here" and "there" to make this opposition explicit.

[71]Cf. J. Lewy, OrNS 29 (1960), 32 note 4.

[72]On this K. Deller, OrNS 31 (1962), 226. Cf. however E. E. Knudsen, OLZ 58 (1963), 353.

[73]Cf. W. von Soden, Linguistica semitica, 44 note 25 and AHw 213b, sub voce *emēdum* "to impose".

[74]On this most recently J. Aro, Die Vokalisierung des Grundstammes im semitischen Verbum (1964), 18-43 and B. Kienast, "Zu den Vokalklassen beim akkadischen Verbum" in Heidelberger Studien zum Alten Orient (1967), 63-85.

[75]Perhaps with A. Poebel, AS 9, 46 to be explained as elision through accent shift from **pitarusum*. Cf. also K. Hecker, AnOr 44 (1968) § 88 a. Sporadically also in OB, cf. on this R. Borger, BAL 107.

[76]Cf. W. von Soden, ZA 53 (1959), 214f.

[77]B. Kienast, "Verbalformen mit Reduplikation im Akkadischen", OrNS 26 (1957), 44-50 and "Weiteres zum R-Stamm im Akkadischen" JCS 15 (1961), 59-61.

[78]Or as denominative from *dinānum* "representation" in the sense of "to assume the status of a representative".

[79]On this W. von Soden, "Der Imperativ von *alākum* 'gehen'", AfO 18 (1957), 121.

[80]Cf. B. Kienast, "Das System der zweiradikaligen Verben im Akkadischen" in ZA 55 (1963), 138-155.

[81]On MB cf. J. Aro, Studien, 40.

[82]Cf. on this W. von Soden, "Ingressiv-durative N-Stämme mediae geminatae", Or NS 20 (1951), 257-266.

[83]Cf. K. Deller, Diss. §22 d-f.

[84]For the final radical of *awûm* see AHw s.v.

[85]See on this R. Borger, BAL 110.

[86]No D stem exists for *nêʾum*; cf. W. von Soden, Or NS 24 (1955), 388f.

[87]See now W. von Soden, BiOr XXIII (1966), 53f.

[88]Cf. W. von Soden, Or NS 25 (1956), 147.

[89]Cf. J. Lewy, "Old Assyrian *izêzum* and its Implications", Or NS 28 (1959), 351-360.

[90]Cf. J. Lewy, WdO II (1959), 434 note 6.

[91]Cf. R. Borger, Or NS 27 (1958), 147.

[92]On this B. Kienast, "Satzeinleitendes *mā* im älteren Akkadischen", ZA 54 (1961), 90-99 and K. Hecker, Diss. [Translator's note: So Matouš; but cf. now Hecker, AnOr 44 (1968) § 106 d and § 130.]

[93]Cf. J. Lewy, Or NS 29 (1960), 29-38.

[94]Cf. D. O. Edzard, Die Kongruenz in akkadischen Personnamen", ZA 55 (1963), 113-130.

[95]Cf. Th. Jacobsen, "*ittallak niāti*" JNES 19 (1960), 100-116 (see most recently "The Akkadian Ablative Accusative", JNES 22 [1963], 18-29) and W. von Soden, "Zum Akkusativ der Beziehung im Akkadischen", Or NS 30 (1961), 156-162.

[96]W. von Soden, "Status rectus-Formen vor dem Genitiv im Akkadischen und die sogenannte uneigentliche Annexion im Arabischen", JNES 19 (1960), 163-171.

[97]Indispensible for this J. Aro, Die Akkadischen Infinitivkonstruktionen (SO XXVI, 1961), reviewed by K. Deller, "Zur Syntax des Infinitivs im nA", Or NS 31 (1962), 225-235.

[98]For the MB cf. J. Aro, Studien, 136ff.

[99]On this see K. Hecker, AnOr 44 (1968) § 144.

[100]For oaths in OA cf. H. Hirsch, WZKM 57 (1961), 49.

PARADIGMS

A. Nouns I-X

Declension of the Masculine (§§38-39)

I	old	middle	new	late
sg. nom.	*šarr-um*[1]	*šarr-u*	*šarr-u*	*šarr-u/i/a*
gen.	*šarr-im*	*šarr-i*[2]	*šarr-i*[2]	*šarr-u/i/a*
acc.	*šarr-am*	*šarr-a*	*šarr-a/u*	*šarr-u/i/a*
pl. nom.	*šarr-ū, šarr-ānu*	*šarr-ū, šarr-ānu*	*šarr-ī/ē*[3], *šarr-āni*	*šarr-ī/ē*[3], *šarr-āni*
gen./acc.	*šarr-ī*[4], *šarr-āni*	*šarr-ī*[4], *šarr-āni*	*šarr-ī/ē*[3], *šarr-āni*	*šarr-ī/ē*[3], *šarr-āni*
dual nom.	*īn-ān*[5]	*īn-ā(n)*[5]	*īn-ān*[6], *īn-ī/ē(n)*[7]	*īn-ān*[6], *īn-ī/ē(n)*[7]
gen./acc.	*īn-īn*[7]	*īn-ī(n)*[7]	*īn-ān*[6], *īn-ī/ē(n)*[7]	*īn-ān*[6], *īn-ī/ē(n)*[7]

1. *šarrum* "king"; **2.** Ass. *šarr-e*; **3.** Ass. *šarr-ē*; **4.** Ass. *šarr-ē* **5.** *īnum* (Ass. *ēnum*) "eye"; **6.** Ass. *ēn-ā(n)*; **7.** Ass. *ēn-ē(n)*.

Declension of the Feminine (§§38-39)

II-III	old	middle	new	late
sg. nom.	*šarr-atum*[1]	*šarr-atu*[2]	*šarr-atu*[2]	*šarr-atu/i/a*[3]
gen.	*šarr-atim*[4]	*šarr-ati*[5]	*šarr-ati*[5]	*šarr-atu/i/a*[3]
acc.	*šarr-atam*	*šarr-ata*	*šarr-ata/u*[2]	*šarr-atu/i/a*[3]
pl. nom.	*šarr-ātum*	*šarr-ātu*	*šarr-āti/e*[6]	*šarr-āte*
gen.-acc.	*šarr-ātim*	*šarr-āti*[6]	*šarr-āti/e*[6]	*šarr-āte*
dual nom.	*šap-tān*[7]	*šap-tā(n)*	*šap-tā(n)*	*šap-tā(n), šap-tī/ē(n)*
gen.-acc.	*šap-tīn*[8]	*šap-tī(n)*[8]	*šap-tī/ē(n)*	*šap-tā(n), šap-tī/ē(n)*

1. *šarratum* "queen"; the *a* of the fem. ending follows Ass. vowel harmony, so *šarrutum*; **2.** Ass. *šarr-utu*; **3.** Ass. *šarr-utu, šarr-ete*; **4.** Ass. *šarr-itim*; **5.** Ass. *šarr-ete*; **6.** Ass. *šarr-āte*; **7.** *šaptum* "lip"; **8.** Ass. *šap-tē(n)*.

Declension of Adjectives (§§38-40)

IV[1]	masc.	fem.	masc.	fem.
sg. nom.	*dann-um*[2]	*dann-atum*	*ell-um*[3]	*ell-etum*[4]
gen.	*dann-im*	*dann-atim*	*ell-im*	*ell-etim*[5]
acc.	*dann-am*	*dann-atam*	*ell-am*	*ell-etam*[6]
pl. nom.	*dann-ūtum*	*dann-ātum*	*ell-ūtum*	*ell-ētum*[7]
gen./acc.	*dann-ūtim*	*dann-ātim*	*ell-ūtim*	*ell-ētim*[8]

1. Here only the forms for OB and OA; those for Middle-, Neo-, and Late-Bab./Ass. are easily formed from Paradigms I-III; **2.** *dannum* "strong"; **3.** *ellum* "pure"; **4.** Ass. *ell-utum*; **5.** Ass. *ell-itim*; **6.** Ass. *ell-atam*; **7.** Ass. *ell-ātum*; **8.** Ass. *ell-ātim*.

Declension of the Noun with Weak Third Radical (§40)

a) Stems in *ā*:

V	old	middle	neo-/late
sg. nom.	*puruss-āʾum/-ûm* [1,2]	*puruss-û*	*puruss-û* [3]
gen.	*puruss-āʾim/-êm* [2]	*puruss-ê*	*puruss-û/ê* [3]
acc.	*puruss-âm*	*puruss-â*	*puruss-û/ê* [3]
pl. nom.	*puruss-āʾū/-û* [2]	*puruss-û*	*puruss-û/ê*
gen./acc.	*puruss-āʾī/-ê* [2]	*puruss-ê*	*puruss-û/ê*

1. *purussûm* "decision"; **2.** Uncontracted forms are OAkk and OA; **3.** NA also uncontracted: *puruss-āʾu/āʾe*.

b) Stems in *i*:

VI	old	middle	neo-	late
masc. sg. nom.	*rabi-um* [1], *rab-ûm*	*rab-û* [2]	*rab-û* [2]	*rab-û/î/â*
gen.	*rab-îm*	*rab-î* [3]	*rab-î*	*rab-û/î/â*
acc.	*rabi-am, rab-âm*	*rab-â* [4]	*rab-â/û* [2]	*rab-û/î/â*
masc. pl. nom.	*rabi-ūtum*	*rab-ûtu* [5]	*rab-ûti/e* [6]	*rab-ûte*
gen./acc.	*rabi-ūtim, rab-ûtim*	*rab-ûti* [6]	*rab-ûti/e* [6]	*rab-ûte*
fem. sg.	*rab-ītum*, etc.	*rab-ītu*, etc.	*rab-ītu*, etc.	*rab-ītu*, etc.
fem. pl.	*rabi-ātum*, etc.; *rab-âtum*	*rab-âtu* etc.	*rab-âti/e* [7]	*rab-âte*

1. *rabûm* "large"; **2.** Ass. *rabi-u*; **3.** Ass. *rab-ê*; **4.** Ass. *rabi-a*; **5.** Ass. *rabi-ūtu*; **6.** Ass. *rabi-ūte*; **7.** Ass. *rabi-āte*.

The Construct State Noun without and with Suffixes (§§41-42)

a) The Masc. Noun in the Sing.

VII	nom.-acc.	gen.	nom.-acc.	gen.
constr. st.	*bēl*[1]	*bēl*[2]	*libbi*[3]	*libbi*
sg. 1 c	*bēl-ī*	*bēlī-ya*	*libbī*	*libbī-ya*
2 m	*bēl-ka*	*bēlī-ka*	*libba-ka*	*libbī-ka*
2 f	*bēl-ki*	*bēlī-ki*	*libba-ki*[4]	*libbī-ki*
3 m	*bēl-šu*[5]	*bēlī-šu*	*libba-šu*[6]	*libbī-šu*
3 f	*bēl-ša*[5]	*bēlī-ša*	*libba-ša*	*libbī-ša*
pl. 1 c	*bēl-ni*	*bēlī-ni*	*libba-ni*[7]	*libbī-ni*
2 m	*bēl-kunu*	*bēlī-kunu*	*libba-kunu*[8]	*libbī-kunu*
2 f	*bēl-kina*	*bēlī-kina*	*libba-kina*[9]	*libbī-kina*
3 m	*bēl-šunu*	*bēlī-šunu*	*libba-šun*[10]	*libbī-šunu*
3 f	*bēl-šina*	*bēlī-šina*	*libba-šina*[11]	*libbī-šina*

1. *bēlum* "lord"; **2.** OAkk *bēli*; **3.** *libbum* "heart"; **4.** Ass. *libbi-ki*; **5.** After dental and sibilant (cf. §20c): *bīs-su*,etc.; **6.** Ass. *libbu-šu*; **7.** Ass. *libbi-ni*; **8.** Ass. *libba-k(u)nu*; **9.** Ass. *libba-k(i)na*; **10.** Ass. *libba-š(u)nu*; **11.** Ass. *libba-š(i)na*.

VII	nom.	gen.	acc.
constr. st.	*būš(i)*[1]	*būš(i)*	*būš(i)*
sg. 1 c	*būš-ī*	*būšī-ya*	*būšā-ya*
2 m	*būšū-ka*	*būšī-ka*	*būšā-ka*
2 f	*būšū-ki*	*būšī-ki*	*būšā-ki*
3 m	*būšū-šu*	*būšī-šu*	*būšā-šu*
3 f	*būšū-ša*	*būšī-ša*	*būšā-ša*
pl. 1 c	*būšū-ni*	*būšī-ni*	*būšā-ni*
2 m	*būšū-kunu*	*būšī-kunu*	*būšā-kunu*
2 f	*būšū-kina*	*būšī-kina*	*būšā-kina*
3 m	*būšū-šunu*	*būšī-šunu*	*būšā-šunu*
3 f	*būšū-šina*	*būšī-šina*	*būšā-šina*

b) The Fem. Noun in the Singular

VIII	nom./acc.	gen.	nom./acc.	gen.
constr. st.	*šallat*[1]	*šallat*[2]	*qīšti*[3]	*qīšti*
sg. 1 c	*šallat-ī*	*šallatī-ya*	*qīšt-ī*	*qīštī-ya*
2 m	*šallat-ka*	*šallatī-ka*	*qīšta-ka*	*qīštī-ka*
2 f	*šallat-ki*	*šallatī-ki*	*qīšta-ki*[4]	*qīštī-ki*
3 m	*šallas-su*	*šallatī-šu*	*qīšta-šu*[5]	*qīštī-šu*
3 f	*šallas-sa*	*šallatī-ša*	*qīšta-ša*	*qīštī-ša*
pl. 1 c	*šallat-ni*	*šallatī-ni*	*qīšta-ni*[6]	*qīštī-ni*
2 m	*šallat-kunu*	*šallatī-kunu*	*qīšta-kunu*[7]	*qīštī-kunu*
2 f	*šallat-kina*	*šallatī-kina*	*qīšta-kina*[8]	*qīštī-kina*
3 m	*šallas-sunu*	*šallatī-šunu*	*qīšta-šunu*[9]	*qīštī-šunu*
3 f	*šallas-sina*	*šallatī-šina*	*qīšta-šina*[10]	*qīštī-šina*

1. *šallatum* "booty, plunder"; **2.** OAkk *šallati*; **3.** *qīštum* "gift"; **4.** Ass. *qīšti-ki*; **5.** Ass. *qīštu-šu*; **6.** Ass. *qīšti-ni*; **7.** Ass. *qīšta-k(u)nu*; **8.** Ass. *qīšta-k(i)na*; **9.** Ass. *qīšta-š(u)nu*; **10.** Ass. *qīšta-š(i)na*.

c) The Noun in the Dual

IX	nom.	gen./acc.
constr. st.	*īn-ā*[1]	*īn-ī*[2]
sg. 1 c	*īnā-ya*[3]	*īnī-ya*[4]
2 m	*īnā-ka*[3]	*īnī-ka*[4]
3 m	*īnā-šu*[3]	*īnī-šu*[4]
pl. 3 m	*īnā-šunu*[3]	*īnī-šunu*[4]

1. *īnum* "eye", Ass. *ēnum*; **2.** Ass. *ēn-ē*; **3.** Ass. *ēnā-ya*,etc.; **4.** Ass. *ēnē-ya*, etc.

d) Nouns in the Plural

X	-ū	-ī	-ānu	-ūtum	-ātum
constr. st.	*šarr-ū*	*šarr-ī*[1]	*(šarr-ānu)*	*dann-ūt*[2]	*šarr-āt*
sg. 1 c	*šarrū-a*[3]	*šarrī/ē-ya*	*šarrānū-a*[3]	*dannūtū-a*[3]	*šarrātū-a*[3]
2 m	*šarrū-ka*	*šarrī/ē-ka*	*šarrānū-ka*	*dannūtū-ka*	*šarrātū-ka*
2 f	*šarrū-ki*	*šarrī/ē-ki*	*šarrānū-ki*	*dannūtū-ki*	*šarrātū-ki*
3 m	*šarrū-šu*	*šarrī/ē-šu*	*šarrānū-šu*	*dannūtū-šu*	*šarrātū-šu*
3 f	*šarrū-ša*	*šarrī/ē-ša*	*šarrānū-ša*	*dannūtū-ša*	*šarrātū-ša*
pl. 1 c	*šarrū-ni*	*šarrī/ē-ni*	*šarrānū-ni*	*dannūtū-ni*	*šarrātū-ni*
2 m	*šarrū-kunu*	*šarrī/ē-kunu*	*šarrānū-kunu*	*dannūtū-kunu*	*šarrātū-kunu*
2 f	*šarrū-kina*	*šarrī/ē-kina*	*šarrānū-kina*	*dannūtū-kina*	*šarrātū-kina*
3 m	*šarrū-šunu*	*šarrī/ē-šunu*	*šarrānū-šunu*	*dannūtū-šunu*	*šarrātū-šunu*
3 f	*šarrū-šina*	*šarrī/ē-šina*	*šarrānū-šina*	*dannūtū-šina*	*šarrātū-šina*

1. Ass. *šarr-ē*, also LB; **2.** *dannum* "strong"; **3.** Also (more rarely) *šarrū-ya*, etc.

Verbs (XI-XXXVII)

The Stative (§54)

XI	*šarrum*	*bēlum*	*parāsum*[1]
sg. 3 m	*šar*	*bēl*	*paris*
3 f	*šarr-at*	*bēl-et*[2]	*pars-at*
2 m	*šarr-āta*[3]	*bēl-ēta*[4]	*pars-āta*[5]
2 f	*šarr-āti*	*bēl-ēti*[4]	*pars-āti*
1 c	*šarr-āku*	*bēl-ēku*[6]	*pars-āku*
dual 3 c[7]	*šarr-ā*	*bēl-ā*	*pars-ā*
pl. 3 m	*šarr-ū*	*bēl-ū*	*pars-ū*
3 f	*šarr-ā*	*bēl-ā*	*pars-ā*
2 m	*šarr-ātunu*	*bēl-ētunu*[8]	*pars-ātunu*
2 f	*šarr-ātina*[9]	*bēl-ētina*	*pars-ātina*
1 c	*šarr-ānu*[10]	*bēl-ēnu*[11]	*pars-ānu*[12]

1. *parāsum* "to divide". **2.** Ass. *bēl-at*; **3.** Ass. *šarr-āti*; **4.** Ass. *bēl-āti*; **5.** Ass. *pars-āti*; **6.** Ass. *bēl-āku*; **7.** Only OAkk and OA; **8.** Ass. *bēl-ātunu*; **9.** Cf. OA *sinniš-ātini*; **10.** Ass. *šarr-āni*; **11.** Ass. *bēl-āni*; **12.** Ass. *pars-āni*.

Present G (§55)

XII	*parāsum*	*paqādum*[1]	*rapādum*[2]	subjunctive	ventive
sg. 3 m	*i-parras*	*i-paqqid*	*i-rappud*	*i-parras-u*[3]	*i-parras-a(m)*
3 f[4]	*ta-parras*	*ta-paqqid*	*ta-rappud*	*ta-parras-u*[5]	*ta-parras-a(m)*
2 m	*ta-parras*	*ta-paqqid*	*ta-rappud*	*ta-parras-u*[5]	*ta-parras-a(m)*
2 f	*ta-parras-ī*[6]	*ta-paqqid-ī*	*ta-rappud-ī*	*ta-parras-ī*[7]	*ta-parras-ī(m)*[8]
1 c	*a-parras*	*a-paqqid*	*a-rappud*	*a-parras-u*[9]	*a-parras-a(m)*
dual 3 c[10]	*i-parras-ā*	*i-paqqid-ā*	*i-rappud-ā*	*i-parras-ā*[11]	*i-parras-āni(m)*
pl. 3 m	*i-parras-ū*[12]	*i-paqqid-ū*	*i-rappud-ū*	*i-parras-ū*[13]	*i-parras-ūni(m)*[14]
3 f	*i-parras-ā*	*i-paqqid-ā*	*i-rappud-ā*	*i-parras-ā*[15]	*i-parras-āni(m)*
2 c	*ta-parras-ā*	*ta-paqqid-ā*	*ta-rappud-ā*	*ta-parras-ā*[16]	*ta-parras-āni(m)*
1 c	*ni-parras*	*ni-paqqid*	*ni-rappud*	*ni-parras-u*[17]	*ni-parras-a(m)*

1. *paqādum* "to entrust"; **2.** *rapādum* "to run"; **3.** Ass. *i-parrus-ūni*; **4.** Only OAkk and OA, otherwise the 3 fs is identical with the 3 ms (cf. §52d note); **5.** Ass. *ta-parrus-ūni*; **6.** Ass. *ta-parris-ī*; **7.** Ass. *ta-parris-īni*; **8.** Ass. *ta-parris-ī(m)*; **9.** Ass. *a-parrus-ūni*; **10.** Only OAkk and OA; **11.** Ass. *i-parras-āni*; **12.** Ass. *i-parrus-ū*; **13.** Ass. *i-parrus-ūni*; **14.** Ass. *i-parrus-ūni(m)*; **15.** Ass. *i-parras-āni*; **16.** Ass. *ta-parras-āni*; **17.** Ass. *ni-parrus-ūni*.

Preterite G (§56)

XIII	*parāsum*	*ṣabātum*[1]	*paqādum*	subjunctive	ventive
sg. 3 m	*i-prus*	*i-ṣbat*	*i-pqid*	*i-prus-u*[2]	*i-prus-a(m)*
3 f[3]	*ta-prus*	*ta-ṣbat*	*ta-pqid*	*ta-prus-u*[4]	*ta-prus-a(m)*
2 m	*ta-prus*	*ta-ṣbat*	*ta-pqid*	*ta-prus-u*[4]	*ta-prus-a(m)*
2 f	*ta-prus-ī*	*ta-ṣbat-ī*[5]	*ta-pqid-ī*	*ta-prus-ī*[6]	*ta-prus-ī(m)*[7]
1 c	*a-prus*	*a-ṣbat*	*a-pqid*	*a-prus-u*[8]	*a-prus-a(m)*
du. 3 c[9]	*i-prus-ā*	*i-ṣbat-ā*	*i-pqid-ā*	*i-prus-ā*[10]	*i-prus-āni(m)*
pl. 3 m	*i-prus-ū*	*i-ṣbat-ū*[11]	*i-pqid-ū*	*i-prus-ū*[12]	*i-prus-ūni(m)*[13]
3 f	*i-prus-ā*	*i-ṣbat-ā*	*i-pqid-ā*	*i-prus-ā*[14]	*i-prus-āni(m)*
2 c	*ta-prus-ā*	*ta-ṣbat-ā*	*ta-pqid-ā*	*ta-prus-ā*[15]	*ta-prus-āni(m)*
1 c	*ni-prus*	*ni-ṣbat*	*ni-pqid*	*ni-prus-u*[16]	*ni-prus-a(m)*

1. *ṣabātum* "to seize"; **2.** Ass. *i-ṣbut-ūni*; **3.** See Parad. XII, note 4; **4.** Ass. *ta-ṣbut-ūni*; **5.** Ass. *ta-ṣbit-ī*; **6.** Ass. *ta-ṣbit-īni*; **7.** Ass. *ta-ṣbit-ī(m)*; **8.** Ass. *a-ṣbut-ūni*; **9.** See Parad. XII, note 10; **10.** Ass. *i-prus-āni*; **11.** Ass. *i-ṣbut-ū*; **12.** Ass. *i-ṣbut-ūni*; **13.** Ass. *i-ṣbut-ūni(m)*; **14.** Ass. *i-prus-āni*; **15.** *ta-prus-āni*; **16.** Ass. *ni-ṣbut-ūni*.

G Perf. (§57), *Imp.* (§59e), *Prec.* (§60a).

XIV	perfect		imp./prec.[1]			ventive
	parāsum	*maqātum* [2]	*parāsum*	*ṣabātum*	*naqādum*	*parāsum*
sg. 3 m	*i-ptaras*	*i-mtaqut*[3]	*li-prus*	*li-ṣbat*	*li-pqid*	*li-prus-a(m)*
3 f[4]	*ta-ptaras*	*ta-mtaqut*[5]	*lū taprus*	*lū taṣbat*	*lū tapqid*	*lū taprus-a(m)*
2 m	*ta-ptaras*	*ta-mtaqut*[5]	*purus*	*ṣabat*	*piqid*	*purs-am*
2 f	*ta-ptars-ī*	*ta-mtaqt-ī*[6]	*purs-ī*	*ṣabt-ī*	*piqd-ī*	*purs-ī(m)*
1 c	*a-ptaras*	*a-mtaqut*[7]	*lu-prus*[8]	*lu-ṣbat*[8]	*lu-pqid*[8]	*lu-prus-a(m)*[8]
du. 3 c[9]	*i-ptars-ā*	*i-mtaqt-ā*[10]				
pl. 3 m	*i-ptars-ū*	*i-mtaqt-ū*[11]	*li-prus-ū*	*li-ṣbat-ū*[12]	*li-pqid-ū*	*li-prus-ūni(m)*
3 f	*i-ptars-ā*	*i-mtaqt-ā*[10]	*li-prus-ā*	*li-ṣbat-ā*	*li-pqid-ā*	*li-prus-āni(m)*
2 c	*ta-ptars-ā*	*ta-mtaqt-ā*[13]	*purs-ā*	*ṣabt-ā*	*piqd-ā*	*purs-āni(m)*
1 c	*ni-ptaras*	*ni-mtaqut*[14]	*i ni-prus*[15]	*i ni-ṣbat*[15]	*i ni-pqid*[15]	*i ni-prus-a(m)*[15]

1. In 3 sg. and pl. prec., in 1 pl. cohortative; **2.** *maqātum* "to fall"; **3.** Ass. *i-mtuqut*; **4.** Cf. Parad. XII, note 4; **5.** Ass. *ta-mtuqut*; **6.** Ass. *ta-mtuqt-ī* (§5e); **7.** Ass. *a-mtuqut*; **8.** Ass. *la-prus*,etc.; **9.** Cf. Parad. XII, note 10; **10.** Ass. *i-mtuqt-ā* (§5c); **11.** Ass. *i-mtuqt-ū*; **12.** Ass. *li-ṣbut-ū*; **13.** Ass. *ta-mtuqt-ā*; **14.** Ass. *ni-mtuqut* ; **15.** Ass. *lū ni-prus*, etc.

Stems of Triradical Strong Verbs (§§ 63–72)

XV	pres.	perf.	pret.	imp.	part.	inf.	verbaladj.	stat.
G a-u	*iparras*	*iptaras*	*iprus*	*purus*	*pārisu(m)*	*parāsu(m)*	*parsu(m)*	*paris*
a-a	*imaḫḫaṣ*[1]	*imtaḫaṣ*	*imḫaṣ*	*maḫaṣ*	*māḫiṣu(m)*	*maḫāṣu(m)*	*maḫṣu(m)*	*maḫiṣ*
i - i	*ipaqqid*	*iptaqid*[2]	*ipqid*	*piqid*	*pāqidu(m)*	*paqādu(m)*	*paqdu(m)*	*paqid*
u -u	*irappud*	*irtapud*[3]	*irpud*	*rupud*	*rāpidu(m)*	*rapādu(m)*	—	—
Gt a-u	*iptarras*	*iptatras*	*iptaras*	*pitras*	*muptarsu(m)*	*pitrusu(m)*[12]	—	*pitrus*
a-a	*imtaḫḫaṣ*	*imtatḫaṣ*	*imtaḫaṣ*	*mitḫaṣ*	*mumtaḫṣu(m)*	*mitḫuṣu(m)*[13]	—	*mitḫuṣ*
i - i	*iptaqqid*	*iptatqid*	*iptaqid*[2]	*pitqid*	*muptaqdu(m)*	*pitqudu(m)*[14]	—	*pitqud*
u-u	*irtaggum*[4]	*irtatgum*	*irtagum*[5]	*ritgum*	*murtagmu(m)*	*ritgumu(m)*[15]	—	*ritgum*
Gtn a-u	*iptanarras*	*iptatarras*	*iptarras*	*pitarras*	*muptarrisu(m)*	*pitarrusu(m)*	—	*pitarrus*
a-a	*imtanaḫḫaṣ*	*imtataḫḫaṣ*	*imtaḫḫaṣ*	*mitaḫḫaṣ*	*mumtaḫḫiṣu(m)*	*mitaḫḫuṣu(m)*	—	*mitaḫḫuṣ*
i - i	*iptanaqqid*	*iptataqqid*	*iptaqqid*	*pitaqqid*	*mumtaqqidu(m)*	*pitaqqudu(m)*	—	*pitaqqud*
u-u	*irtanappud*	*irtatappud*	*irtappud*	*ritappud*	*murtappidu(m)*	*ritappudu(m)*	—	*ritappud*
D	*uparras*	*uptarris*	*uparris*	*purris*[6]	*muparrisu(m)*	*purrusu(m)*[16]	*purrusu(m)*[16]	*purrus*[17]
Dt	*uptarras*	*uptatarris*	*uptarris*	*putarris*	*muptarrisu(m)*	*putarrusu(m)*	—	—
Dtn	*uptanarras*	*uptatarris*	*uptarris*	*putarris*	*muptarrisu(m)*	*putarrusu(m)*	—	*putarrus*
Š	*ušapras*	*uštapris*	*ušapris*	*šupris*[7]	*mušaprisu(m)*	*šuprusu(m)*[18]	*šuprusu(m)*[18]	*šuprus*[19]
Št^1	*uštapras*	*uštatapris*	*uštapris*	*šutapris*	*muštaprisu(m)*	*šutaprusu(m)*	*šutaprusu(m)*	*šutaprus*
Št^2	*uštaparras*	*uštatapris*	*uštapris*	*šutapris*	*muštaprisu(m)*	*šutaprusu(m)*	—	—
Štn	*uštanapras*	*uštatapris*	*uštapris*	*šutapris*	*muštaprisu(m)*	*šutaprusu(m)*	—	—
N a-u	*ipparras*	*ittapras*	*ipparis*[8]	*napris*	*mupparsu(m)*	*naprusu(m)*	*naprusu(m)*	*naprus*
a-a	*immaḫḫaṣ*	*ittamḫaṣ*	*immaḫiṣ*[9]	*namḫiṣ*	*mummaḫṣu(m)*	*namḫuṣu(m)*	*namḫuṣu(m)*	*namḫuṣ*
i - i	*ippaqqid*	*ittapqid*	*ippaqid*[10]	*napqid*	*muppaqdu(m)*	*napqudu(m)*	*napqudu(m)*	*napqud*
u-u	*(immaggur)*[11]	*(ittamgur)*	*(immagur)*	—	*mummagru(m)*	*namguru(m)*	*namguru(m)*	*namgur*
Ntn a-u	*ittanapras*	*(ittatapras)*	*ittapras*	*itapras*	*muttaprisu(m)*	*ittaprusu(m)*	—	*itaprus*
i – i	*ittanapqid*	*(ittatapqid)*	*ittapqid*	*itapqid*	*muttapqidu(m)*	*ittapqudu(m)*	—	*itapqud*
R	*upararras*	—	*upararris*	—	—	—	—	—
Rt	*uptararras*	—	*uptararris*	*putararris*	*muptararrisu(m)*	*putararrusu(m)*	—	—
ŠD	*ušparras*	—	*ušparris*	*šuparris*	*mušparrisu(m)*	*šuparrusu(m)*	—	—

1. *maḫāṣum* "to strike"; **2.** Ass. *iptiqid*; **3.** Ass. *irtupud*; **4.** *ragāmum* "to bring charges"; **5.** Ass. *irtugum*; **6.** Ass. *parris*; **7.** Ass. *šapris*; **8.** Ass. *ippiris*; **9.** Ass. *immiḫiṣ*; **10.** Ass. *ippiqid*; **11.** *magārum* "to be favorably inclined, propitious"; **12.** Ass. *pitarsu(m)*; **13.** *mitaḫṣu(m)*; **14.** Ass. *pitaqdu(m)*; **15.** Ass. *ritagmu(m)*; **16.** Ass. *parrusu(m)*; **17.** Ass. *parrus*; **18.** Ass. *šaprusu(m)*; **19.** Ass. *šaprus*.

Stems of Quadriliteral Verbs (§73)

A. The Š-Group

XVI	Pres.	perf.	pret.	imp.	part.	inf.	verbal-adj.	stat.
a) G	*išqallal*[1] (*ušqallal*)	*uštaqallil*	*ušqallil*	*šuqallil*	(*mušqallilum*)	*šuqallulu(m)*	—	(*šuqallul*)
Gt	*uštaqlal*	(*uštataqlil*)	*ušaqlil*	—	—	—	—	—
b) G	*uškên*[2]	(*uštekēn*)[3]	*uškē/īn*[4]	—	*muškē/īnu(m)*	*šukênu(m)*	—	—
Gt	*uštepêl*[5]	—	*uštepēl*	—	—	—	—	—

B. The N-Stem-Class

XVII	pres.	perf.	pret.	imp.	part.	inf.	verbaladj.	stat.
N	*ibbalakkat*[6] (*ibbalakkit*)	*ittabalkat* (*ittabalkit*)	*ibbalkit*	(*nabalkit*)	*mubbalkitu(m)*	*nabalkutu(m)*, *nablakutu(m)*	*nabalkutu(m)*	*nabalkut*
Ntn	*ittanablakkat*	*ittatablakkat*	*ittabalakkat*	—	*muttablakkitu(m)*	*itablakkutu(m)*	—	—
Š	*ušbalakkat*	*uštabalkit*	*ušbalkit*	*šubalkit*	*mušbalkitu(m)*	*šubalkutu(m)*	*šubalkutu(m)*	*šubalkut*
Št	(*uštabalkat*)	(*uštatabalkit*)	(*uštabalkit*)	—	(*muštabalkitum*)	*šutabalkutum*	—	—
Štn	*uštanablakkat*	—	*uštablakkit*	—	(*muštablakkitum*)	*šutablakkutum*	—	(*šutablakkut*)

1. *šuqallulum* "to hang"; **2.** *šukênum* "to prostrate oneself", Ass. *uškân*; **3.** OA (*uštaka*ʾʾ*in*); MA *ultaka*ʾʾ*in*; **4.** Ass. *uška*ʾʾ*in*; **5.** *šupêlum* "to exchange"; **6.** *nabalkutum* "to transgress".

Initial Aleph Verbs (§75), *a*-Class (Group I), G-stem

XVIII	pres.	perf.	pret.	imp./prec.[1]
sg. 3 m	*iḫḫaz*[2]	*ītaḫaz*[3]	*īḫuz*[4]	*līḫuz*[5]
3 f[6]	*taḫḫaz*	*tātaḫaz*	*tāḫuz*	*lū tāḫuz*
2 m	*taḫḫaz*	*tātaḫaz*	*tāḫuz*	*aḫuz*
2 f	*taḫḫazī*[7]	*tātaḫzī*	*tāḫuzī*	*aḫzī*
1 c	*aḫḫaz*	*ātaḫaz*	*āḫuz*	*lūḫuz*[8]
pl. 3 m	*iḫḫazū*[9]	*ītaḫzū*[10]	*īḫuzū*[11]	*līḫuzū*[12]
3 f	*iḫḫazā*[13]	*ītaḫzā*[14]	*īḫuzā*[15]	*līḫuzā*[16]
2 c	*taḫḫazā*	*tātaḫzā*	*tāḫuzā*	*aḫzā*
1 c	*niḫḫaz*[17]	*nītaḫaz*[18]	*nīḫuz*[19]	*i nīḫuz*[20]

1. Cf. Parad. XIV, note 1; **2.** *aḫāzum* "to seize"; Ass. *eḫḫaz*; **3.** Ass. *ētaḫaz*; **4.** Ass. *ēḫuz*; **5.** Ass. *lēḫuz*; **6.** Cf. Parad. XII, note 4; **7.** Ass. *taḫḫizī*; **8.** Ass. *lāḫuz*; **9.** Ass. *eḫḫuzū*; **10.** Ass. *ētaḫzū*; **11.** Ass. *ēḫuzū*; **12.** Ass. *lēḫuzū*; **13.** Ass. *eḫḫazā*; **14.** Ass. *ētaḫzā*; **15.** Ass. *ēhuzā*; **16.** Ass. *lēḫuzā*; **17.** Ass. *neḫḫaz*; **18.** Ass. *nētaḫaz*; **19.** Ass. *nēḫuz*; **20.** Ass. *lū nēḫuz*.

Initial Aleph Verbs (§75), *e*-Class (Group II)

XIX	pres.	perf.	pret.	imp./prec.[1]
sg. 3 m	*irrub*[2]	*īterub*[3]	*īrub*[4]	*līrub*[5]
3 f[6]	*terrub*[7]	*tēterub*[8]	*tērub*	*lū tērub*
2 m	*terrub*[9]	*tēterub*[10]	*tērub*	*erub*
2 f	*terrubī*[11]	*tēterbī*[12]	*tērubī*	*erbī*
1 c	*errub*[13]	*ēterub*[14]	*ērub*	*lūrub*[15]
pl. 3 m	*irrubū*[16]	*īterbū*[17]	*īrubū*[18]	*līrubū*[19]
3 f	*irrubā*[20]	*īterbā*[21]	*īrubā*[22]	*līrubā*[23]
2 c	*terrubā*[24]	*tēterbā*[25]	*tērubā*	*erbā*
1 c	*nirrub*[26]	*nīterub*[27]	*nīrub*[28]	*i nīrub*[29]

1. Cf. Parad. XIV, note 1; **2.** *erēbum* "to enter"; Ass. *errab*; **3.** Ass. *ētarab*; **4.** Ass. *ērub*; **5.** Ass. *lērub*; **6.** Cf. Parad. XII, note 4; **7.** Ass. *terrab*; **8.** Ass. *tētarab*; **9.** Ass. *terrab*; **10.** Ass. *tētarab*; **11.** Ass. *terribī*; **12.** Ass. *tētarbī*; **13.** Ass. *errab*; **14.** Ass. *ētarab*; **15.** Ass. *lērub*; **16.** Ass. *errubū*; **17.** Ass. *ētarbū*; **18.** Ass. *ērubū*; **19.** Ass. *lērubū*; **20.** Ass. *errabā*; **21.** Ass. *ētarbā*; **22.** Ass. *ērubā*; **23.** Ass. *lērubā*; **24.** Ass. *terrabā*; **25.** Ass. *tētarbā*; **26.** Ass. *nerrab*; **27.** Ass. *nētarab*; **28.** Ass. *nērub*; **29.** Ass. *lū nērub*.

Stems of Initial Aleph Verbs (*a*-Class) (§75)

XX	pres.	perf.	pret.	imp.	part.	inf.	verbaladj.	stat.
G a-u	*iḫḫaz*[1]	*ītaḫaz*[2]	*īḫuz*[3]	*aḫuz*	*āḫizu(m)*	*aḫāzu(m)*	*aḫzu(m)*	*aḫiz*
a-a	*ibbal*[4]	*ītabal*[5]	*ībal*[6]	*abal*	*ābilu(m)*	*abālu(m)*	*ablu(m)*	*abil*
i - i	*irrim*[7]	*ītarim*[8]	*īrim*[9]	*arim*	*ārimu(m)*	*arāmu*	*armu*	*arim*
u-u	*ikkuš*[10]	*ītakuš*[11]	*īkuš*[12]	*akuš*	*ākišu(m)*	*akāšu(m)*	—	—
Gt	*ītaḫḫaz*[13]	(*ītatḫaz*[14])	*ītaḫaz*[15]	*atḫaz*	—	*atḫuzu(m)*[22]	—	(*atḫuz*)
Gtn	*ītanaḫḫaz*[16]	*ītataḫḫaz*[17]	*ītaḫḫaz*[18]	*ataḫḫaz*	*mūtaḫḫizu(m)*	*ataḫḫuzu(m)*	—	(*ataḫḫuz*)
D	*uḫḫaz*	*ūtaḫḫiz*	*uḫḫiz*	*uḫḫiz*[19]	*muḫḫizu(m)*	*uḫḫuzu(m)*[23]	*uḫḫuzu(m)*[23]	*uḫḫuz*[24]
(strong)	*uʾabbat*[20]	(*uʾtabbit*)	(*uʾabbit*)	*ubbit*	*muʾabbitu(m)*	*ubbutu(m)*	*ubbutu(m)*	*ubbut*
Dt	*ūtaḫḫaz*	*ūtataḫḫiz*	*ūtaḫḫiz*	(*utaḫḫiz*)	(*mūtaḫḫizum*)	(*utaḫḫuzum*)	—	—
Dtn	(*ūtanaḫḫaz*)	(*ūtataḫḫiz*)	(*ūtaḫḫiz*)	(*utaḫḫiz*)	(*mūtaḫḫizum*)	(*utaḫḫuzum*)	—	(*utaḫḫuz*)
Š	*ušaḫḫaz*	*uštāḫiz*	*ušāḫiz*	*šūḫiz*[21]	*mušāḫizu(m)*	*šūḫuzu(m)*[25]	*šūḫuzu(m)*[25]	*šūḫuz*[26]
Št	*uštaḫḫaz*	*uštatāḫiz*	*uštāḫiz*	*šutāḫiz*	*muštāḫizu(m)*	*šutāḫuzu(m)*	—	*šutāḫuz*
Štn	*uštanaḫḫaz*	(*uštataḫḫiz*)	*uštaḫḫiz*	*šutaḫḫiz*	*muštaḫḫizu(m)*	*šutaḫḫuzu(m)*	—	*šutaḫḫuz*
N	*innaḫḫaz*	*ittanḫaz*	*innaḫiz*	*nanḫiz*	*munnaḫzu(m)*	*nanḫuzu(m)*	*nanḫuzu(m)*	*nanḫuz*
	iʾʾabbat	*ittaʾbat*	*iʾʾabit*	—	—	(*naʾbutum*)	(*naʾbutum*)	(*naʾbut*)
Ntn	*ittanaḫḫaz*	—	(*ittaḫḫaz*)	—	—	—	—	—

1. Ass. *eḫḫaz*; **2.** Ass. *ētaḫaz*; **3.** Ass. *ēḫuz*; **4.** *abālum* "to dry"; Ass. *ebbal*; **5.** Ass. *ētabal*; **6.** Ass. *ēbal*; **7.** *arāmu* "to cover"; Ass. *errim*; **8.** Ass. *ētirim*; **9.** Ass. *ērim*; **10**. *akāšum* "to go"; Ass. *ekkuš*; **11.** Ass. *ētukuš*; **12.** Ass. *ēkuš*; **13.** Ass. *ētaḫḫaz*; **14.** Ass. *ētatḫaz*; **15.** Ass. *ētaḫaz*; **16.** Ass. *ētanaḫḫaz*; **17.** Ass. *ētataḫḫaz*; **18.** Ass. *ētaḫḫaz*; **19** Ass. *aḫḫiz*; **20.** *abātum* D "to destroy"; **21.** Ass. *šāḫiz*; **22.** Ass. *ataḫzu(m)*; **23.** Ass. *aḫḫuzu(m)*; **24.** Ass. *aḫḫuz*; **25.** Ass. *šāḫuzu(m)*; **26.** Ass. *šāḫuz*.

Stems of Initial Aleph Verbs (*e*-class) (§75)

XXI	pres.	perf.	pret.	imp.	part.	inf.	verbaladj.	stat.
G a–u	*ippeš*[1]	*ītepeš*[2]	*īpuš*[3]	*epuš*	*ēpišu(m)*	*epēšu(m)*[23]	*epšu(m)*	*epiš*
	ippuš	*ītepuš*						
i – i	*ittiq*[4]	*ītetiq*[5]	*ītiq*[4]	*etiq*	*ētiqu(m)*	*etēqu(m)*[24]	—	*etiq*
u – u	*irrub*[7]	*īterub*[8]	*īrub*[9]	*erub*	*ēribu(m)*	*erēbu(m)*[25]	—	*erib*
Gt	*(īteppuš)*	*(ītetpuš)*	*(ītepuš)*	*(etpuš)*	—	*(etpušum)*	—	*(etpuš)*
Gtn	*ītenepppeš*[10]	*īteteppuš*[11]	*īteppuš*[12]	*eteppeš*[13]	*mūteppišu(m)*	*iteppušu(m)*[26]	—	*eteppuš*[27]
	īteneppuš			*eteppuš*				
D	*uppaš*	*ūteppiš*[14]	*uppiš*	*uppiš*[15]	*muppišu(m)*	*uppušu(m)*[28]	*uppušu(m)*[28]	*uppuš*[29]
Dt	*(ūteppeš)*[16]	*(ūteteppiš)*	*(ūteppiš)*[17]	—	*(mūteppišum)*	*uteppušu(m)*[30]	—	—
Dtn	*(ūteneppeš)*	*(ūteteppiš)*	*(ūteppiš)*	—	*(mūteppišum)*	*uteppušu(m)*[30]	—	*(uteppuš)*[31]
Š	*ušeppeš*[18]	*uštēpiš*	*ušēpiš*	*šūpiš*[19]	*mušēpišu(m)*	*šūpušu(m)*[32]	*šūpušu(m)*[32]	*šūpuš*[33]
Št	*(ušteppeš)*	*uštetēpiš*	*uštēpiš*	*(šutēpiš)*	*muštēpišu(m)*	*šutēpušu(m)*	—	*šutēpuš*
Štn	*ušteneppeš*	*(ušteteppiš)*	*(ušteppiš)*	*(šuteppiš)*	*mušteppišu(m)*	*(šuteppušum)*	—	*(šuteppuš)*
N	*inneppeš*[20]	*(ittenpeš)*[21]	*innepiš*[22]	—	*munnepšu(m)*	*(nenpušum)*	—	*(nenpuš)*
	inneppuš	*ittenpuš*	*innepuš*					
Ntn	*(ittenenpeš)*	—			—	—	—	

1. *epēšum* "to make, do"; Ass. *eppaš*; **2.** Ass. *ētapaš*; **3.** Ass. *ēpuš*; **4.** *etēqum* "to go by"; Ass. *ettiq*; **5.** Ass. *ētitiq*; **6.** Ass. *ētiq*; **7.** *erēbum* "to enter"; Ass. *errab*; **8.** Ass. *ētarab*; **9.** Ass. *ērub*; **10.** Ass. *ētanappaš*; **11.** Ass. *(ētatappaš)*; **12.** Ass. *ētappaš*; **13.** Ass. *(etappaš)*; **14.** Ass. *ūtappiš*; **15.** Ass. *eppiš*; **16.** Ass. *ūtappaš*; **17.** Ass. *ūtappiš*; **18.** Ass. *ušeppaš*; **19.** Ass. *šēpiš*; **20.** Ass. *inneppaš*; **21.** Ass. *ittēpaš*; **22.** Ass. *innipiš*; **23.** Ass. *epāšu(m)*; **24.** Ass. *etāqu(m)*; **25.** Ass. *erābu(m)*; **26.** Ass. *etappušu(m)*; **27.** Ass. *etappuš*; **28.** Ass. *eppušu(m)*; **29.** Ass. *eppuš*; **30.** Ass. *utappušu(m)*; **31.** Ass. *(utappuš)*; **32.** Ass. *šēpušu(m)*; **33.** Ass. *šēpuš*.

Stems of Medial Aleph Verbs (§76)

XXII	pres.	perf.	pret.	imp.	part.	inf.	verbaladj.	stat.
G Gr. I	*išâl*[1]	*ištāl*	*išāl*	*šāl*	*šāʾilu(m)*	*šâlu(m)*	—	*šaʾil*
strong	*iraʾʾub*[2]	*irtaʾub*	*irʾub*	*(ruʾub)*	*rāʾibu*	*raʾābu*	*raʾbu*	*raʾib*
Gr. II	*ibêl*[3]	*ibtēl*	*ibēl*	*bēl*	*(bēʾilum)*	*bêlu(m)*	*bēlu(m)*	*bēl*
strong (Ass.)	*ibeʾʾal*	*ibteʾal*	*ibʾel*	*(*beʾil)*	—	*beʾālu(m)*	*bēlu(m)*	*bēl*
Gt	*ištâl*	*ištatāl*	*ištāl*	*šitāl*	*muštālu(m)*	*šitūlu(m)*	—	*šitūl*
Gtn	*ištanaʾʾal*	*(ištataʾʾal)*	*ištaʾʾal*	*šitaʾʾal*	*(muštaʾʾilum)*	*šitaʾʾulu(m)*	—	*(šitaʾʾul)*
D	*ušâl*	*uštaʾʾil*	*ušaʾʾil*	*šuʾʾil*	*mušaʾʾilu(m)*	*šûlu(m)*	*šûlu(m)*	*(šûl)*
Š	*(ušmâd)*[4]	*(uštamīd)*	*(ušmīd)*	*(šumīd)*	—	*šumūdu(m)*	*(šumūdum)*	*(šumūd)*
N Gr. I	*iššâl*	—	*iššāl*	—	*(muššālum)*	—	—	—
Gr. II	*ibbêl*	—	*ibbēl*	—	*(mubbēlum)*	—	—	—

1. *šâlum* "to question"; **2.** *râbu* "to become angry"; **3.** *bêlum* "to rule"; **4.** *mâdum* "to be many, much".

Verbs with Initial n (§78)

XXIII	pres.	perf.	pret.	imp./prec.[1]
sg. 3 m	*inaqqar*[2]	*ittaqar*	*iqqur*	*liqqur*
3 f[3]	*tanaqqar*	*tattaqar*	*taqqur*	*lū taqqur*
2 m	*tanaqqar*	*tattaqar*	*taqqur*	*uqur*
2 f	*tanaqqarī*	*tattaqrī*	*taqqurī*	*uqrī*
1 c	*anaqqar*	*attaqar*	*aqqur*	*luqqur*[4]
pl. 3 m	*inaqqarū*	*ittaqrū*	*iqqurū*	*liqqurū*
3 f	*inaqqarā*	*ittaqrā*	*iqqurā*	*liqqurā*
2 c	*tanaqqarā*	*tattaqrā*	*taqqurā*	*uqrā*
1 c	*ninaqqar*	*nittaqar*	*niqqur*	*i niqqur*[5]

1. See Parad. XIV, note 1; **2.** *naqārum* "to tear down"; **3.** See Parad. XII, note 4; **4.** Ass. *laqqur*; **5.** Ass. *lū niqqur*.

Stems of Initial n *Verbs* (§75)

XXIV	pres.	perf.	pret.	imp.	part.	inf.	verbaladj.	stat.
G	*inaqqar*	*ittaqar*	*iqqur*	*uqur*	*nāqiru(m)*	*naqāru(m)*	*naqru(m)*	*naqer*
	inaddin[1]	*ittadin*[2]	*iddin*	*idin*[3]	*nādiru(m)*[7]	*nadānu(m)*[8]	*nadnu(m)*[9]	*nadin*[10]
Gt	*(ittaqqar)*	*(ittatqar)*	*(ittaqar)*	—	*(muttaqrum)*	*itaṭlum*[11]	*(itqurum)*	*(itqur)*
Gtn	*ittanaqqar*	*ittataqqar*	*ittaqqar*	*itaqqar*	*muttaqqiru(m)*	*itaqquru(m)*	—	*itaqqur*
D	*unaqqar*	*uttaqqer*	*unaqqer*	*nuqqer*[4]	*munaqqiru(m)*	*nuqquru(m)*[11]	*nuqquru(m)*[11]	*nuqqur*[12]
Dt	*uttaqqar*	*(uttataqqer)*	*uttaqqer*	—	*(muttaqqirum)*	*(n)utaqquru(m)*	—	—
Dtn	*uttanaqqar*	*(uttataqqer)*	*uttaqqer*	—	*muttaqqiru(m)*	*(n)utaqquru(m)*	—	*(n)utaqqur*
Š	*ušaqqar*	*uštaqqer*	*ušaqqer*	*šuqqer*[5]	*mušaqqiru(m)*	*šuqquru(m)*[13]	*šuqquru(m)*[13]	*šuqqur*[14]
Št[1]	*uštaqqar*	*(uštataqqer)*	*uštaqqer*	—	*muštaqqiru(m)*	*šutaqquru(m)*	—	—
Št[2]	*uštanaqqar*	*(uštataqqer)*	*uštaqqer*	*(šutaqqer)*	*muštaqqiru(m)*	*šutaqquru(m)*	*(šutaqqurum)*	*šutaqqur*
Štn	*uštanaqqar*	*uštataqqer*	*uštaqqer*	*(šutaqqer)*	*muštaqqiru(m)*	*šutaqquru(m)*	—	*šutaqqur*
N	*innaqqar*	*ittanqar*	*innaqer*[6]	*(naqqer)*	*munnaqru(m)*	*nanquru(m)*	*nanquru(m)*	*nanqur*
Ntn	*(ittanaqqar)*	—	*ittanqar*	*(itaqqar)*	—	*itaqquru(m)*	—	*itaqqur*

1. *nadānum* "to give"; Ass. *iddan*; **2.** Ass. *ittidin*; **3.** Ass. *din*; **4.** Ass. *naqqer*; **5.** Ass. *šaqqer*; **6.** Ass. *inneqer*; **7.** Ass. *tādinu(m)*; **8.** Ass. *tadānu(m)*; **9.** Ass. *tadnu(m)*; **10.** Ass. *tadin*; **11.** OA "to look at each other"; **12.** Ass. *naqquru(m)*; **13.** Ass. *naqqur*; **14.** Ass. *šaqquru(m)*; **15.** *šaqqur*.

Verbs with Initial w(a)- (§80)
G-stem

XXV	pres.	perf.	pret.	imp./prec.[1]	stat.
sg. 3 m	*uššab*[2]	*ittašab*[3]	*ūšib*	*līšib*[4]	*(w)ašib*[5]
3 f[6]	*tuššab*	*tattašab*	*tūšib*	*lū tūšib*	*(w)ašbat*[7]
2 m	*tuššab*	*tattašab*	*tūšib*	*šib*[8], *tišab*	*(w)ašbāta*[9]
2 f	*tuššabī*[10]	*tattašbī*	*tušbī*	*šibī*[11]	*(w)ašbāti*[12]
1 c	*uššab*	*attašab*	*ūšib*	*lūšib*	*(w)ašbāku*[13]
pl. 3 m	*uššabū*[14]	*ittašbū*	*ūšibū, ušbū*	*lišbū*[15]	*(w)ašbū*[16]
3 f	*uššabā*	*ittašbā*	*ūšibā, ušbā*	*lišbā*[17]	*(w)ašbā*[18]
2 c	*tuššabā*	*tattašbā*	*tūšibā, tušbā*	*šibā*[19], *tišbā*	(m.) *(w)ašbātunu*[20], (f.) *(w)ašbātina*[21]
1 c	*nuššab*	*nittašab*	*nūšib*	*i nūšib*[22]	*(w)ašbānu*[23]

1. See Parad. XIV, note 1; **2.** *(w)ašābum* "to sit down"; **3.** NA *ittūšib*, etc.; **4.** Ass. *lūšib*; **5.** Ass. *ušib*; **6.** See Parad. XII, note 4; **7.** Ass. *ušbat*; **8.** Ass. also *tašab*; **9.** Ass. *ušbāti*; **10.** Ass. *tuššibī*; **11.** Ass. also *tašbī*; **12.** Ass. *ušbāti*; **13.** Ass. *ušbāku*; **14.** Ass. *uššubū*; **15.** Ass. *lušbū*; **16.** Ass. *ušbū*; **17.** Ass. *lušbā*; **18.** Ass. *ušbā*; **19.** OB and Ass. also *tašbā*; **20.** Ass. *ušbātunu*; **21.** Ass. *(ušbātini)*; **22.** Ass. *lū nūšib*; **23.** Ass. *ušbāni*.

Verbs with Initial y (§81)
G-stem

XXVI	pres.	perf.	pret.	imp./prec.[1]	stat.
sg. 3 m	*inniq*[2]	*īteniq*[3]	*īniq*	*līniq*	*eniq*
3 f[4]	*tenniq*	*tēteniq*[5]	*tēniq*	*lū tēniq*	*enqet*[6]
2 m	*tenniq*	*tēteniq*[5]	*tēniq*	*eniq*	*enqēta*[7]
2 f	*tenniqī*	*tētenqī*[8]	*tēniqī*	*enqī*	*enqēti*[9]
1 c	*enniq*	*ēteniq*[10]	*ēniq*	*lûniq*[11]	*enqēku*[12]
pl. 3 m	*inniqū*	*ītenqū*[10]	*īniqū*	*līniqū*	*enqū*
3 f	*inniqā*	*ītenqā*[13]	*īniqā*	*līniqā*	*enqā*
2 c	*tenniqā*	*tētenqā*[14]	*tēniqā*	*enqā*	m. *enqētunu*[15] f. *enqētina*[16]
1 c	*ninniq*	*nīteniq*[17]	*nīniq*	*i nīniq*[18]	*enqēnu*[19]

1. See Parad. XIV, note 1; **2.** *enēqum* "to suck"; **3.** Ass. *ītiniq*; **4.** See Parad. XII, note 4; **5.** Ass. *tētiniq*; **6.** Ass. *enqat*; **7.** Ass. *enqāti*; **8.** Ass. *(tētinqī?)*; **15.** Ass. *enqātunu*; **16.** Ass. *(enqātini)*; **17.** Ass. *nītiniq*; **18.** Ass. *lū nīniq*; **19.** Ass. *enqāni*.

Stems of I w(a)- *and I* y *Verbs* (§§80–81)

XXVII	pres.	perf.	pret.	imp.	part.	inf.	verbaladj.	stat.
G I *w(a)*-	*ubbal*[1]	*ittabal*[2], *itbal*	*ūbil*	*bil*	*bābilu(m)*	*(b)abālu(m)*	—	*babil*
I *y*	*inniq*[1a]	*īteniq*	*īniq*	*eniq*	*ēniqu(m)*	*enēqu(m)*[10]	*(enqum)*	*eniq*
Gt I *w(a)*-	*ittabbal*	*(ittatbal)*	*itbal*	*tabal*	*(muttablum)*	*(itbulum)*	*(itbulum)*	*(itbul)*
I *y*	*(ītenniq)*	*(ītetniq)*	*(īteniq)*	*(etniq)*	*(mūtenqum)*	*(itnuqum)*	*(itnuqum)*	*(itnuq)*
Gtn I *w(a)*-	*ittanabbal*	*(ittatabbal)*	*ittabbal*	*itabbal*	*muttabbilu(m)*	*itabbulu(m)*	—	*(itabbul)*
I *y*	*ītenenniq*	*(ītetenniq)*	*ītenniq*	*(ētenniq)*	*(mūtenniqum)*	*(etennuqum)*	—	*(etennuq)*
D I *w(a)*-	*uwaššar*[3]	*ūtaššer*	*uwaššer*	*wuššer*[4]	*muwašširu(m)*	*(w)uššuru(m)*[11]	*(w)uššuru(m)*[11]	*(w)uššur*[12]
I *y*	*uṣṣar*[5]	*ūteṣṣer*	*uṣṣer*	*uṣṣer*	*muṣṣiru(m)*	*uṣṣuru(m)*	*uṣṣuru(m)*	*uṣṣur*
Dt I *w(a)*-	*ūtaššar*	*(ūtataššer)*	*ūtaššer*	—	*mūtašširu(m)*	*(utaššurum)*	—	—
I *y*	*ūteṣṣer*	*(ūteteṣṣer)*	*ūteṣṣer*	—	*mūteṣṣiru(m)*	*uteṣṣuru(m)*	—	—
Dtn I *w(a)*-	*(ūtanaššar)*	*(ūtataššer)*	*(ūtaššer)*	*utaššer*	*mūtašširu(m)*	*(utaššurum)*	—	*(utaššur)*
Š I *w(a)*-	*ušabbal*	*uštābil*	*ušābil*	*šūbil*[6]	*mušābilu(m)*	*šūbulu(m)*[13]	*šūbulu(m)*[13]	*šūbul*[14]
I *y*	*ušenneq*[7]	*uštēniq*	*ušēniq*	*šūniq*[8]	*mušēniqu(m)*	*šūnuqu(m)*[15]	*šūnuqu(m)*[15]	*šūnuq*[16]
Št I *w(a)*-	*uštabbal*	*(uštatābil)*	*uštābil*	*šutābil*	*muštābilu(m)*	*šutābulu(m)*	*šutābulu(m)*	*šutābul*
I *y*	*(uštenneq)*	*(uštetēniq)*	*(uštēniq)*	*(šutēniq)*	*(muštēniqum)*	*(šutēnuqum)*	*(šutēnuqum)*	*(šutēnuq)*
Štn I *w(a)*-	*uštānabbal*, *uštēnebbel*	*(uštatabbil*, *uštetebbil)*	*(ušt$^{a/e}$bbil)*	*(šut$^{a/e}$bbil)*	*(mušt$^{a/e}$bbilum)*	*(šut$^{a/e}$bbulum)*	—	*(šut$^{a/e}$bbul)*
N I *w(a)*-	*iwwallad*[9], *iʾʾallad*, *ibbabbal*	*(ittawlad?)*	*iwwalid*, *iʾʾalid*, *ibbabil*	—	*(muwwaldum)*	—	—	—
I *y*	*(inneṣṣer)*	—	*(inneṣer)*	—	*(munneṣrum)*	*(nēṣurum)*	—	*nēṣur*
Ntn I *w(a)*-	—	—	—	*(nēṣer)*	—	—	—	—
I *y*	*(itteneṣṣer)*	—	*(itteṣṣer)*	—	*(mutteṣṣirum)*	—	—	—

1. *(w)abālum* "to carry"; **1a**. *enēqum* "to suck"; **2.** NA *ittūbil*; **3.** *(w)ašārum* "to release"; **4.** Ass. *waššer*; **5.** *eṣērum* "to draw"; **6.** Ass. *šābil*; **7.** Ass. *ušēnaq*; **8.** Ass. *šēniq*; **9.** *(w)alādum* "to give birth"; **10.** Ass. *enāqu(m)*; **11.** Ass. *waššuru(m)*; **12.** Ass. *waššur*; **13.** Ass. *šēbulu(m)*; **14.** Ass. *šēbul*; **15.** Ass. *šēnuqu(m)*; **16.** Ass. *šēnuq*.

Middle Weak Verbs (§82)
b) II *ū*, G- and D-stems

XXX	G pres.	G perf.	G pret.	G imp./prec.[1]	D pres.	D pret.	D imp./prec.[1]
sg. 3 m	*ikân*[2]	*iktūn*[3]	*ikūn*	*likūn*	*ukān*[4]	*ukīn*[5]	*likīn*[6]
3 f[7]	*takân*[8]	*taktūn*[9]	*takūn*	*lū takūn*	*tukān*[10]	*tukīn*	*lū tukīn*[11]
2 m	*takân*[8]	*taktūn*[9]	*takūn*	*kūn*	*tukān*[10]	*tukīn*	*kīn*[12]
2 f	*takunnī*	*taktūnī*	*takūnī*	*kūnī*	*tukannī*	*tukinnī*	*kinnī*
1 c	*akân*[13]	*aktūn*[14]	*akūn*	*lukūn*[15]	*ukān*[16]	*ukīn*[5]	*lukīn*[6]
pl. 3 m	*ikunnū*	*iktūnū*	*ikūnū*	*likūnū*	*ukannū*	*ukinnū*	*likinnū*[17]
3 f	*ikunnā*	*iktūnā*	*ikūnā*	*likūnā*	*ukannā*	*ukinnā*	*likinnā*[17]
2 c	*takunnā*	*taktūnā*	*takūnā*	*kūnā*	*tukannā*	*tukinnā*	*kinnā*
1 c	*nikân*[18]	*niktūn*[19]	*nikūn*	*i nikūn*[20]	*nukān*[21]	*nukīn*	*i nukīn*[22]

1. See Parad. XIV, note 1; **2.** *kânum* "to be true"; Ass. *ikūan*; **3.** Ass. *iktūan*; **4.** Ass. *ukân*; **5.** Ass. *uka''in*, etc.; **6.** Ass. *luka''in*, etc.; **7.** See Parad. XII, note 4; **8.** Ass. *takūan*; **9.** Ass. *taktūan*; **10.** Ass. *tukân*; **11.** Ass. *lū tuka''in*; **12.** Ass. *ka''in*, etc.; **13.** Ass. *akūan*; **14.** Ass. *aktūan*; **15.** Ass. *lakūn*; **16.** Ass. *ukân*; **17.** Ass. *luka''in*$^{\bar{u}}$*/ā*; **18.** Ass. *nikūan*; **19.** Ass. *niktūan*; **20.** Ass. *lū nikūn*; **21.** Ass. *nukân*; **22.** Ass. *lū nuka''in*.

Middle Weak Verbs (§82)
a) II *ā* and II *ī*, G-stem

XXVIII-XXIX	II *ā* pres.	II *ā* pret.	II *ā* imp./prec.	II *ī* pres.	II *ī* perf.	II *ī* pret.	II *ī* imp./prec.[1]
sg. 3 m	*ibâš*[2]	*ibāš*	*libāš*	*iqīaš*[3], *iqâš*	*iqtīš*[4]	*iqīš*	*liqīš*
3 f[5]	*tabâš*	*tabāš*	*lū tabāš*	*taqīaš*, *taqâš*	*taqtīš*[6]	*taqīš*	*lū taqīš*
2 m	*tabâš*	*tabāš*	*bāš*	*taqīaš*, *taqâš*	*taqtīš*[6]	*taqīš*	*qīš*
2 f	*tabašši*	*tabāši*	*bāšī*	*taqiššī*	*taqtīšī*	*taqīšī*	*qīšī*
1 c	*abâš*	*abāš*	*lubāš*[7]	*aqīaš*, *aqâš*	*aqtīš*[8]	*aqīš*	*luqīš*[9]
pl. 3 m	*ibaššū*	*ibāšū*	*libāšū*	*iqiššū*	*iqtīšū*	*iqīšū*	*liqīšū*
3 f	*ibaššā*	*ibāšā*	*libāšā*	*iqiššā*	*iqtīšā*	*iqīšā*	*liqīšā*
2 c	*tabaššā*	*tabāšā*	*bāšā*	*taqiššā*	*taqtīšā*	*taqīšā*	*qīšā*
1 c	*nibâš*	*nibāš*	*i nibāš*[10]	*niqīaš*, *niqâš*	*niqtīš*[11]	*niqīš*	*i niqīš*[12]

1. See Parad. XIV, note 1; **2.** *bašûm* "to be ashamed"; **3.** *qiāšum*, *qâšum* "to give"; **4.** Ass. *iqtīaš*; **5.** See Parad. XII, note 4; **6.** Ass. *taqtīaš*; **7.** Ass. *labāš*; **8.** Ass. *aqtīaš*; **9.** Ass. *laqīš*; **10.** Ass. *lū nibāš*; **11.** Ass. *niqtīaš*; **12.** Ass. *lū niqīš*.

Stems of the Middle Weak Verbs (§82)

XXXI	pres.	perf.	pret.	imp.	part.	inf.	verbaladj.	stat.
G II *a*	*ibâš*	*ibtāš*	*ibāš*	*bāš*	*bāʾišu(m)*	*bâšu(m)*	—	*bāš*
II *ī*	*iqīaš*, *iqâš*	*iqtīš*[1]	*iqīš*	*qīš*	*qāʾišu(m)*	*qiāšu(m)*, *qâšu(m)*	*qīšu(m)*[17]	*qīš*[18]
II *ū*	*ikân*[2]	*iktūn*[3]	*ikūn*	*kūn*	*dāʾiku(m)*	*kânu(m)*[19]	*kīnu(m)*[20]	*kīn*[21]
Gt II *ī*	(*iqtīaš*?)	—	(*iqtīš*)	—	(*muqtīšum*)	(*qitūšum*)	—	(*qitūš*)
II *ū*	(*iktân*?)[3]	—	(*iktūn*)	—	(*muktīnum*)	(*kitūnum*)	—	(*kitūn*)
Gtn II *ī*	*iqtanīš*[4]	—	(*iqtayyiš?*)	—	—	(*qitayyušum?*)	—	—
II *ū*	*iktanân*[5]	—	(*iktūn?*)	—	—	*kitayyunu(m)*	—	—
D	*ukān*[6]	*uktīn*[7]	*ukīn*[8]	*kīn*[9]	*mukinnu(m)*[22]	*kunnu(m)*[23]	*kunnu(m)*[23]	*kūn*[24]
Dt	*uktān*[10]	(*uktatīn*)[11]	*uktīn*[12]	—	*muktinnu(m)*[25]	*kutunnu(m)*[26]	—	—
Dtn	*uktanān*[14]	(*uktatīn*)[11]	*uktīn*[12]	(*kutīn?*)[13]	*muktinnu(m)*[25]	*kutunnu(m)*[26]	—	*kutūn*[27]
Š	*ušdāk*[15]	*uštadīk*	*ušdīk*	(*šudīk*)	*mušdīku(m)*	*šudūku(m)*[28]	—	*šudūk*
Št	(*uštadāk*)	(*uštatadīk*?)	(*uštadīk*)	(*šutadīk?*)	(*muštadīkum*)	*šutadūku(m)*	—	(*šutadūk*)
N II *ī*	*iqqīaš*, *iqqâš*	—	(*iqqīš*)	—	—	—	—	—
II *ū*	*iddâk*[16]	—	(*iddīk?*)	—	(*muddīkum?*)	(*nadūkum?*)	—	(*nadūk?*)

1. Ass. *iqtīaš*; **2.** Ass. *ikūan*; **3.** Ass. *iktūan*; **4.** Ass. *iqtanīaš*; **5.** Ass. *iktunūan*; **6.** Ass. *ukân*; **7.** Ass. *uktaʾʾin*; **8.** Ass. *ukaʾʾin*; **9.** Ass. *kaʾʾin*; **10.** Ass. *uktân*; **11.** Ass. *uktataʾʾin*; **12.** Ass. *uktaʾʾin*; **13.** Ass. *kutaʾʾin*; **14.** Ass. *uktanân*; **15.** Ass. *dâkum* "to kill"; **16.** Ass. *iddūak*; **17.** Ass. *qēšu(m)*; **18.** Ass. *qēš*; **19.** Ass. *kuānu(m)*; **20.** Ass. *kēnu(m)*; **21.** Ass. *kēn*; **22.** Ass. *mukaʾʾinu(m)*; **23.** Ass. *kaʾʾinu(m)*; **24.** Ass. *kaʾʾun*; **25.** Ass. *muktaʾʾinu(m)*; **26.** Ass. *kutaʾʾunu(m)*; **27.** Ass. *kutaʾʾun*; **28.** SB *šumuttu*, NA *šamuttu* "to kill" (cf. § 82 i).

G-Stem of Final Weak Verbs (§83)
a) III *ī*

XXXII	pres.	perf.	pret.	imp./prec.[1]	stat.	pret. subj.
sg. 3 m	*ibanni*[2]	*ibtani*[3]	*ibni*	*libni*	*bani*	*ibnû*[4]
3 f[5]	*tabanni*	*tabtani*[6]	*tabni*	*lū tabni*	*baniat*[7], *banât*	*tabnû*[8]
2 m	*tabanni*	*tabtani*[6]	*tabni*	*bini*	*baniāta*[9], *banâta*	*tabnû*[8]
2 f	*tabannî*	*tabtanî*[10]	*tabnî*	*binî*[11]	*baniāti*[9], *banâti*	*tabnî*[12]
1 c	*abanni*	*abtani*[13]	*abni*	*lubni*[14]	*baniāku*[15], *banâku*	*abnû*[16]
pl. 3 m	*ibanniu, ibannû*	*ibtaniū*[17], *ibtanû*	*ibniū, ibnû*	*libniū. libnû*	*baniū*[18], *banû*	*ibnû*[19]
3 f	*ibanniā, ibannâ*	*ibtaniā*[20], *ibtanâ*	*ibniā, ibnâ*	*libniā, libnâ*	*baniā*[21], *banâ*	*ibniā*[22], *ibnâ*
2 c	*tabanniā. tabannâ*	*tabtaniā*[23], *tabtanâ*	*tabniā. tabnâ*	*biniā*[24], *binâ*	(m) *baniātunu*[25], *banâtunu*; (f) *baniātina*[26], *banâtina*	*tabniā*[27], *tabnâ*
1 c	*nibanni*	*nibtani*[28]	*nibni*	*i nibni*[29]	*baniānu*[30], *banânu*	*nibnû*[31]

1. See Parad. XIV, note 1; **2.** *banûm* "to build"; **3.** Ass. *ibtini*; **4.** Ass. *ibniūni*; **5.** See Parad. XII, note 4; **6.** Ass. *tabtini*; **7.** Ass. also *banʾat*; **8.** Ass. *tabniūni*; **9.** Ass. *baniāti, banʾāti*; **10.** Ass. *tabtinî*; **11.** Ass. *binʾī*; **12.** Ass. *tabnî-ni*; **13.** Ass. *abtini*; **14.** Ass. *labni*; **15.** Ass. also *banʾāku*; **16.** Ass. *abniūni*; **17.** Ass. *ibtiniū, ibtanʾū*; **18.** Ass. also *banʾū*; **19.** Ass. *ibiū-ni*; **20.** Ass. *ibtiniā, ibtanʾā*; **21.** Ass. also *banʾā*; **22.** Ass. *ibniā-ni*; **23.** Ass. *tabtiniā, tabtanʾā*; **24. Ass.** *binʾā*; **25.** Ass. also *banʾātunu*; **26.** Ass. also *banʾātina*; **27.** Ass. *tabniā-ni*; **28.** Ass. *nibtini*; **29.** Ass. *lū nibni*; **30.** Ass. *baniāni, banʾāni*; **31.** Ass. *nibniūni*.

b) III *ē*

XXXIII	pres.	perf.	pret.	imp./prec.[1]	stat.
sg. 3 m	*išemme*[2]	*išteme*	*išme*	*lišme*	*šemi*
3 f[3]	*tešemme*[4]	*tešteme*[5]	*tešme*[6]	*lū tešme*[7]	*šemiat, šemât*[8]
2 m	*tešemme*[4]	*tešteme*[5]	*tešme*[6]	*š^{i}/eme*	*šemiāta, šemâta*[9]
2 f	*tešemm$^{\hat{i}/\hat{e}}$*[10]	*teštem$^{\hat{i}/\hat{e}}$*[11]	*tešm$^{\hat{i}/\hat{e}}$*[12]	*šim$^{\hat{i}/\hat{e}}$*[12a]	*šemiāti, šemâti*[9]
1 c	*ešemme*[13]	*ešteme*[14]	*ešme*[15]	*lušme*[16]	*šemiāku, šemâku*[17]
pl. 3 m	*išemmû*[18]	*ištemû*[19]	*išmû*[20]	*lišmû*[21]	*šemû*[22]
3 f	*išemmeā*[23], *išemmâ*	*ištemeā*[24], *ištemâ*	*išmeā, išmâ*	*lišmeā, lišmâ*	*šemiā*[25], *šemâ*
2 c	*tešemmeā*[26], *tešemmâ*	*teštemeā*[27], *teštemâ*	*tešmeā*[28], *tešmâ*	*šimiā*[29]	(m) *šemiātunu*[30], *šemâtunu*; (f) *šemiātina, šemâtina*
1 c	*nišemme*[31]	*ništeme*[32]	*nišme*	*i nišme*[33]	*šemiānu, šemânu*[34]

1. See Parad. XIV, note 1; **2.** *šemûm* "to hear"; Ass. *išamme*; **3.** See Parad. XII, note 4; **4.** Ass. *tašamme*; **5.** Ass. *tašteme*; **6.** Ass. *tašme*; **7.** Ass. *lū tašme*; **8.** Ass. *šamʾat*; **9.** Ass. *šamʾāti*; **10.** Ass. *tašamm$^{\hat{i}/\hat{e}}$* **11.** Ass. *taštamʾī*, but *taltiqî* "you have taken"; **12.** Ass. *tašm$^{\hat{i}/\hat{e}}$*; **13.** Ass. *(šimʾī)*; **14.** Ass. *ašteme*; **15.** Ass. *ašme*; **16.** Ass. *lašme*; **17.** Ass. *šamʾāku*; **18.** Ass. *išammeū*; **19.** Ass. *ištamʾū*; **20.** Ass. *išmeū*; **21.** Ass. *lišmeū*; **22.** Ass. *šamʾū*; **23.** Ass. *išammeā*; **24.** Ass. *ištamʾā*; **25.** Ass. *šamʾā*; **26.** Ass. *tašammeā*; **27.** Ass. *taštamʾā*; **28.** Ass. *tašmeā*; **29.** Ass. *šamʾā*; **30.** Ass. *šamʾātunu*; **31.** Ass. *nišamme*; **32.** Ass. *ništeme*; **33.** Ass. *lū nišme*; **34.** Ass. *šamʾāni*.

c) III *ā* and III *ū*

XXXIV–XXXV	III *ā* pres.	III *ā* imp./prec.[1]	III *ū* pres.	III *ū* imp./prec.[1]	III *ū* stat.
sg. 3 m	*ikalla*[2]	*likla*	*imannu*[3]	*limnu*	*manu*
3 f[4]	*takalla*	*lū takla*	*tamannu*	*lū tamnu*	*manât*[5]
2 m	*takalla*	*kila*	*tamannu*	*munu*	*manâta*[6]
2 f	*takallî*	*kilî*[7]	*tamannî*[8]	*munî*[9]	*manâti*[6]
1 c	*akalla*	*lukla*[10]	*amannu*	*lumnu*[11]	*manâku*[12]
pl. 3 m	*ikallû*	*liklû*	*imannû*	*limnû*	*manû*
3 f	*ikallâ*	*liklâ*	*imannâ*[13]	*limnâ*[14]	*manâ*[15]
2 c	*takallâ*	*kilâ*[16]	*tamannâ*[17]	*munâ*[18]	(m.) *manâtunu*[19]
1 c	*nikalla*	*i nikla*[20]	*nimannu*	*i nimnu*[21]	*manânu*[22]

1. See Parad. XIV, note 1; **2.** *kalûm* "to hold back"; **3.** *manûm* "to count"; **4.** See Parad. XII, note 4; **5.** Ass. *manuat*; **6.** Ass. *manuāti*; **7.** Ass. *kilʾī*; **8.** Ass. *tamannuī*; **9.** Ass. *munuī*; **10.** Ass. *lakla*; **11.** Ass. *lamnu*; **12.** Ass. *manuāku*; **13.** Ass. *immanuā*; **14.** Ass. *limnuā*; **15.** Ass. *manuā*; **16.** Ass. *kilʾā*; **17.** Ass. *tamannuā*; **18.** Ass. *munuā*; **19.** Ass. *manuātunu*; **20.** Ass. *lū nikla*; **21.** Ass. *lū nimnu*; **22.** Ass. *manuāni*.

Stems of the Final Weak Verbs (§83)

XXXVI	pres.	perf.	pret.	imp.	part.	inf.	verbaladj.	stat.
G III ā	*ikalla*	*iktala*	*ikla*	*kila*	*kālû(m)*[13]	*kalû(m)*[14]	*kalû(m)*[15]	*kali*
III ē	*išemme*[1]	*išteme*	*išme*[2]	*š^{i}/eme*	*šēmû(m)*[16]	*šemû(m)*[17]	*šemû(m)*[18]	*šemi*[19]
III ī	*ibanni*	*ibtani*[3]	*ibni*	*bini*	*bānû(m)*[20]	*banû(m)*[21]	*banû(m)*[22]	*bani*
III ū	*imannu*	*imtanu*[4]	*imnu*	*munu*	*mānû(m)*[23]	*manû(m)*[24]	*manû(m)*	*manu*
Gt III ī	*ibtanni*	*ibtatni*	*ibtani*[5]	*bitni*	*mubtanû(m)*[25]	*bitnû(m)*[26]	—	*bitni*
Gtn III ī	*ibtananni*[6]	*(ibtatanni)*	*ibtanni*	*bitanni*	*mubtannû(m)i*[27]	*bitannû(m)*[28]	—	*bitannu*
D III ī	*ubanna*[7]	*ubtanni*	*ubanni*	*bunni*[8]	*mubannû(m)*[29]	*bunnû(m)*[30]	*bunnû(m)*[30]	*bunnu*[31]
D III ē	*upette*[9]	*uptett^{i}/e*	*upett^{i}/e*	*putt^{i}/e*	*mupettû(m)*	*puttû(m)*	*puttû(m)*	*puttu*
Dt III ī	*ubtanna*	*ubtatanni*	*ubtanni*	—	*mubtannû(m)*[32]	—	—	—
Dtn III ī	*ubtananna*	*(ubtatanni)*	*ubtanni*	*butanni*	*mubtannû(m)*[32]	—	—	*(butannu)*
Š III ī	*ušabna*	*uštabni*	*ušabni*	*šubni*[10]	*mušabnû(m)*[34]	*šubnû(m)*[35]	*šubnû(m)*[35]	*šubnu*[36]
Št	*uštabna*	*(uštatabni)*	*uštabni*	*(šutabni)*	*muštabnû(m)*[37]	—	—	*(šutabnu)*
Štn	*uštanabna*	*(uštatabni)*	*uštabni*	*(šutabni)*	*muštabnû(m)*[37]	—	—	*šutabnu*
N III ī	*ibbanni*[11]	*ittabni*	*ibbani*[12]	*nabni*	*mubbanû(m)*[39]	—	—	*nabni*
Ntn	*ittanabni*	*(ittatabni)*	*ittabni*	—	*muttabnû(m)*[41]	—	—	—

1. Ass. *išamme*; **2.** OAkk *išma'*; **3.** Ass. *ibtini*; **4.** Ass. *imtunu*; **5.** Ass. *ibtini*; **6.** III *ā: iktanalla*, etc.; III *ē: ištenemme* (Ass. *ištanamme*), etc.; III *ū: imtanannu*, etc.; **7.** *banûm* "to be good", in D "to make good"; **8.** Ass. *banni*; **9.** *petûm* "to open", in Š "to make arable"; similarly Štn *uštenepte*, etc.; **10.** Ass. *šabni*; **11.** III *ā: ikkalla*, etc.; III *ē: iššemmi, ippette* (Ass. *ippatte*), etc.; III *ū: immannu*, etc.; similarly Ntn III *ā: ittanakla*, etc.; **12.** Ass. *ibbini*; **13.** Ass. *kāliu(m)*; **14.** Ass. *kalā'u(m)*; **15.** Ass. *kaliu(m)*; **16.** Ass. *šāmiu(m)*; **17.** Ass. *šamā'u(m)*; **18.** Ass. *šamiu(m)*; **19.** Ass. *šame*; **20.** Ass. *bāniu(m)*; **21.** Ass. *banā'u(m)*; **22.** Ass. *baniu(m)*; **23.** Ass. *māniu(m)*; **24.** Ass. *manā'u(m)*; **25.** Ass. *mubtaniu(m)*; **26.** Ass. *bitnu'u(m)*; **27.** Ass. *mubtanniu(m)*; **28.** Ass. *bitannu'u(m)*; **29.** Ass. *mubanniu(m)*; **30.** Ass. *bannu'u(m)*; **31.** Ass. *bannu*; **32.** Ass. *mubtanniu(m)*; **33.** Ass. *butannu'u(m)*; **34.** Ass. *mušabniu(m)*; **35.** Ass. *šabnu'u(m)*; **36.** Ass. *šabnu*; **37.** Ass. *muštabniu(m)*; **38.** Ass. *šutabnu'u(m)*; **39.** Ass. *mubbaniu(m)*; **40.** Ass. *nabnu'u(m)*; **41.** Ass. *muttabniu(m)*; **42.** Ass. *itabnu'u(m)*.

Verb with Suffixes (§87)

a) with dative suffixes

XXXVII	*išpura(m)*[1]	*išpurūni(m)*[2]	*tašpuri(m)*[3]
sg. 1 c	*išpur-a(m)*	*išpurūni(m)*	*tašpurī-(m)*
2 m	*išpur-akku(m)*	*išpurū-nikku(m)*	—
2 f	*išpur-akki(m)*	*išpurū-nikki(m)*	—
3 m	*išpur-aššu(m)*	*išpurū-niššu(m)*	*tašpuri-ššu(m)*
3 f	*išpur-ašši(m)*	*išpurū-nišši(m)*	*tašpuri-šši(m)*
pl. 1 c	*išpur-anniāši(m)*[4]	*išpurū-niāši(m)*[5]	*tašpuri-nniāši(m)*[6]
2 m	*išpur-akkunūši(m)*[7]	*išpurū-nikkunūši(m)*[8]	—
2 f	*išpur-akkināši(m)*[9]	*išpurū-nikkināši(m)*[10]	—
3 m	*išpur-aššunūši(m)*[11]	*išpurū-niššunūši(m)*[12]	*tašpuri-ššunūši(m)*[13]
3 f	*išpur-aššināši(m)*[14]	*išpurū-niššināši(m)*[15]	*tašpuriššināši(m)*[16]

1. "He sent here"; **2.** "They sent here"; **3.** "You (fem. sg.) sent here"; **4.** Ass. *išpur-niāti*; **5.** Ass. *išpurū-niāti* **6.** Ass. *tašpurī-niāti*; **7.** Ass. *išpur-akkunūti*; **8.** Ass. *išpurū-nikkunūti*; **9.** Ass. *išpur-akkināti*; **10.** Ass. *išpurū-nikkināti*; **11.** Ass. *išpur-šunūti*; **12.** Ass. *išpurū-šunūti*; **13.** Ass. *tašpurī-šunūti*; **14.** Ass. *išpur-šināti*; **15.** Ass. *išpurū-šināti*; **16.** Ass. *tašpurī-šināti.*

b. with accusative suffixes

XXXVIII	*uballiṭ*	*uballiṭū*[2]	*išqul*[3]
sg. 1 c	*uballiṭ-anni*[4]	*uballiṭū-ninni*[5]	*išqul-anni*
2 m	*uballiṭ-ka*	*uballiṭū-ka*	*išqul-ka*
2 f	*uballiṭ-ki*	*uballiṭū-ki*	*išqul-ki*
3 m	*uballis-su*[6]	*uballiṭū-šu*	*išqul-šu*
3 f	*uballis-si*[6]	*uballiṭū-ši*	*išqul-ši*
pl. 1 c	*uballiṭ-niāti*	*uballiṭū-niāti*	*išqul-niāti*
2 m	*uballiṭ-kunūti*[7]	*uballiṭū-kunūti*[7]	*išqul-kunūti*[7]
2 f	*uballiṭ-kināti*[8]	*uballiṭū-kināti*[8]	*išqul-kināti*[8]
3 m	*uballis-sunūti*[6,9]	*uballiṭū-šunūti*[9]	*išqul-šunūti*[9]
3 f	*uballis-sināti*[6,10]	*uballiṭū-šināti*[10]	*išqul-šināti*[10]

1. "He makes to live"; **2.** "They make alive"; **3.** "He weighed out"; **4.**Ass. *uballiṭ-ni*, OA also *uballiṭ-ī*; **5.** Ass. *uballiṭū-ni*; **6.** *-su, -si* etc. according to §20c; **7.** Ass. *uballiṭ-kunu*, etc.; **8.** Ass. *uballiṭ-kina*, etc.; **9.** Ass. *uballits-sunu*, etc.; **10.** Ass. *uballis-sina*, etc.

INDEX OF FORMS AND WORDS

The alphabetization follows the Latin alphabet,=. In addition, ʾ is considered the first letter, *ṣ* follows *s*, and *ṭ* follows *t*. The verbs are not listed in the inf. of the G-stem, as in AHw and CAD, but as roots. Such roots are marked with prefixed *. Mimation (§18c) and internal ʾ — except in the verbs II ʾ (§76) — are disregarded for purposes of alphabetization. The numbers refer to the paragraphs/sections of the grammar, not to pages.

ʾ as a phoneme 4 e; 6 a; 9 a; 13 b; 14 a–d; 18 b; 22 b; 75; 76; 80 c, k; 81 a; 83 a; 84; 85 c
*ʾ*bb* 105 b
*ʾ*bl* Parad. XX
*ʾ*br* 52 f; 75 h
*ʾ*bt* I 14 a; 75 b, d, g; Parad. XX
*ʾ*bt* II 7 a; 14 c; 75 g
*ʾ*dd* 79 a
*ʾ*dr* 75 g
*ʾ*ḫr* 75 d
*ʾ*ḫz* 36 j; 75 b, f; 107 c; 112 b; Parad. XVIII, XX
*ʾ*kl* 14 a, d; 36 a; 75 b, e; 80 i; 87 c; 106 a
*ʾ*km* 114 a
*ʾ*kš* 75 e; Parad. XX
*ʾ*lī* 71 b; 84 b; 85 c
*ʾ*lk* 14 c; 57 b; 58 a; 59 d; 60 c; 67 d; 75 b, e; 80 c; 87 b; 99 b; 105 a, d; 108 a, b; 109 b, h; 112 d; 115 c, e; 116
*ʾ*md* 62b; 109 a
*ʾ*mī* 84 c
*ʾ*mq* 18 e; 108 a
*ʾ*mr* 10; 60 c; 75 g; 100 c; 109 h; 111 a; 115d, e; 116
*ʾ*nḫ* 69 b
*ʾ*nī* 84 b; 111 a
*ʾ*nn* 85 d
*ʾ*pī* 84 b
*ʾ*pl* 106 a; 111 a; 114 d
*ʾ*pš* 5 a; 6 a; 20 c; 33; 60 c; 66 a; 75 h; 114 b; 116; Parad. XXI
*ʾ*rb* 5 a; 17 a; 60 d; 74 e; 75 h, j; 109 b; 111 a; 115 e; 117; Parad. XIX, XXI
*ʾ*rk* 10; 65 f
*ʾ*rm* Parad. XX
*ʾ*rš* 4 e; 20 c; 63 b; 75 h; 109 d
*ʾ*tq* 5 e; Parad. XXI
*ʾ*wū* 84 c
*ʾ*zb* 25 f; 75 h, j; 87 e

a as a vowel 4 a, e; 5 a–c; 6 a, c; 9 a; 61 a; 64 a; 82 b; 85 c
a- 52 d, f
-a (ventive), s. *-a(m)*
-a (*â* constr. st.) 42 f, g
ā (root vowel) 82 b; 84 k; 85 c
-ā (absolute st.) 43 a
-ā (verbal ending) 52 b–d, g
-ā- 52 c
abīlum 17 c
abnum 109 g
abum 17 c; 35 a; 36 b; 38 g 42 h; 100 b; 115 e
abūbum 45 c
abutu 12 b
Abu-waqar 39 b

-išum 90 e
itti 88 c
ittum 88 c

y as a phoneme 4 c; 9 a; 13 a, b; 42 b; 80 a, g; 81; 84 a, g, h
**y*ʾ*l* 3 m; 84 h
-ya 3 a; 13 b; 18 b; 26 b; 42 b; 88 c
yaʾnu/yānu 86 b
yâša 25 d
yâšim 13 a; 25 c
yâšu 25 d
yât 27 c
yâti 13 a; 25 c, e, f
yattum/n 27 b
yāum 13 a; 27 b, c
**yd*ʾ 84 i; 86 a; 118
**yg*$^{\bar{\imath}}/_{\bar{u}}$ 84 h
**ynq* 81 a; Parad. XXVI, XXVII
**yṣp* 81 a
**yṣr* 81 a, b; Parad. XXVII
**yšr* 13 a, b; 69 b; 81 a, c; 109 h
**yšū* 84 i; 86 a

k as a phoneme 4 c, f; 18 e; 21 a
-ka 26 b; 87 b, f; 89 a
kabtum 101 b
kalâma/u 34
kalbatum 36 c; 37 c
kalbum 11 a; 35 a; 36 a; 41 e; 43 e
kalûm 34; 41 c; 42 g; 46 b; 104 c
kanīkum 36 d
Kaniš 112 d
kar(a)šu 104 b
karāšu 3 h
karṣum 64 f
kārum 43 c; 100 c
kaspum 41 c; 43 d; 100 b; 102 b; 106 a; 109 c; 112 b, e;114 a, d; 115 b; 116; 119
kāšidum 36 d
kâšim 16 b; 25 c, e; 88 b
kâšina 25 d
kâšu 25 d
kâšunu 25 d
kâti 25 c
kâtina 25 d
kattum 27 b
kêm 9 a
kēna 99 a
kēnum 105 e
-ki 26 b
kī 88 b; 89 c; 93 a; 94 c, d; 109 h; 112 e; 115 c; 117; 118
kiʾam/kâm 9 a; 93 b
-kīam/-kam 90 k
kibrum 107 a
kilall$^{\bar{a}}/_{\bar{u}}$*n* 47 g
kilattān 47 g
kilīlum 102 b
-kim 26 b; 87 b
kīma 25 e; 45 c; 88 b; 94 c, d; 109 h; 115 a, c; 118
-kina 26 b, c
kināšim 25 c
-kināšim 26 b
kināti 25 c
-kināti 26 b, c; 87 c
k i s a l 36 m
kisalluḫum 36 m
kišādum 36 d
kiššatum 41 d
kittum 37 b; 98 a; 103 d

ni- 52 d
-ni 26 b; 87 c; 105 d
-ni (subj.) 59 d; 96; 114 a, c; 117
niāʾum 27 b
niāšim 25 c
-niāšim 26 b
niāti 9 a; 25 c; 105 d
-niāti 26 b
Nibas 104 a
**nīl* 85 b
-nim 26 b; 58 a, c; 87 b
nīnu 25 c
Ninurta 19 e
nīrum 101 b
nišû 109 h α
**nkl* 46 a
**nks* 78 c
**nmš* 78 f
**npḫ* 109 b
**npš* 78 c
**nqī* 84 e
**nqr* 78 b, c; Parad. XXIII, XXIV
**nsḫ* 109 h
**nsq* 69 b
**nṣr* 28; 54 c
**nšʾ* 36 j; 42 g; 54 d; 58 a; 84 e
**nṭl* 78 c; Parad. XXIV
**nṭū* 109 e
nu- 52 d
-nu 26 c
nubattum 36 h
**nūḫ* 82 g; 84 d; 111 a
nûm 27 b
nuttum 27 b
nūrum 4 a
**nzq* 78 b
**nzr* 74 e

n̊ as a phoneme 16 c; 22 c; 74 e; 78 b
o as a vowel 4 a

p as a phoneme 4 c; 17 b; 20 d
paglum 101 c
pagrum 28
pāna 46 a; 55 b
pānium 48 a
pānum 89 b; 108 b
parakkum 41 i
parasrab 49
patium 101 c
**plḫ* 52 g; 55 b; 60 e; 63 e; 67 b, c
**pls* 66 c, d; 70 d
**pnū* 83 e
**pqd* 1 b; 51 a; 63 b–e; Parad. XII-XV
**prʾ* 83 i
**prs* passim; Parad. XI-XV
**pršd* 73 c
**pšḫ* 63 a
**pšr* 109 g
**ptʾ* 83 b, f, h; 103 a; 115 e; 118; Parad. XXXVI
**pṭr* 68 b
pulḫum 37 e
puluḫtum 37 e; 106 b
pûm 5 d; 49; 89 c
puriddu 41 h
purussûm 1 b; 36 1; 42 g; Parad. V
pūtum 89 b
**pzr* 72 a

q as a phoneme 4 c, f; 15 d; 18 e; 21 a, b; 74 g

tâm$^{t}/_{d}$u 15 d
-tan- 62 b; 70; 73 c; 64 f
tappûm 26 c; 41 h
tapšuḫtum 36 j
tarbītum 109 h
Tāribum 39 c
tarbaṣum 36 j
tarṣu 89 c
taššītum 36 j
**tb*ʾ 54 d; 83 b
**tbl* 33; 80 b
**tdn* 78 d; 109 f
te- 52 f
têrtum 5 b; 117
tērubtum 36 j
tešīt(*um*) 47 b, c
Tiāmat 104 b
**tīl* 85 b
tiš$^{e}/_{i}$t 47 b
tišītum 47 b
tišûm 47 b; 48 b
**ti$^{z}/_{s}$* 85 a
**tkl* 63 e
**tmā* 83 a, b, d
**tmḫ* 6 b
**trū* 83 e; 87 e; 115 b
**tšb* 80 e
tu- 52 d
**tūr* 12 e; 60 e; 82 d, g, h; 87 b; 109 g; 115 b

ṭ as a phoneme 4 c, f; 15 d; 21 a; 74 f, g; 87 d
ṭābtum 37 b
ṭābum 37 b; 45 d
ṭēḫi 89 b
ṭēmum 18 e; 114 b; 115 c
**ṭīb* 60 a; 82 f; g; 105 d; 87 e; 116
**ṭrd* 15 d; 57 a; 64 e; 74 f; 87 e; 111 a
ṭuppum 5 b; 11 b; 26 c; 29 a; 36 m; 41 d; 87 c; 100 c; 106 a; 109 h; 114 c; 115 c, d

u as a phoneme 4 a; 5 c; 9 a, c; 12 a, c; 13 a, b
u 97
u- 52 d, g; 64 a; 65 a; 71 a; 80 c
-u 59 c
ū 97
ū (root vowel) 82 a, 84 d
û 97
-ū (pl.) 38 e; 39 e; 41 i; 42 i; 52 b, d
ūʾa 99 a
ubānum 107 b
ugbabtum 109 e
Uišdiš 114 a
ukultum 41 g
ul(*a*) 98 b; 100 b, d; 109 d, e; 118
ulla 92 b
ullīkīʾam 29 d
ullûm 29 d; 90 b
ultu 89 a; 92 b; 94 c; 115 c
ulū 97
-um (loc.-adv.) 18 d; 39 a;
-um (nom.) 39 b; 40 a; 44; 90 c; 109 d
-ûm 36 1
umma 95; 100 b
ummānum 3 i; 31; 39 e
ummum 36 b; 37 i
ūmum 10; 19 b; 29 c; 45 b;
46 a; 90 a; 107 a, c; 115 d
unūtum 33
Ur 3 h